A Certain Measure

A Certain Measure

AN INTERPRETATION OF
PROSE FICTION

BY ELLEN GLASGOW

NEW YORK

HARCOURT, BRACE AND COMPANY

Contents

v

FOREWORD

IT WOULD appear, from the best examples, that the proper way of beginning a preface to one's work is with a humble apology for having written at all. But humility, as I have had frequent occasion to observe, is a hypocritical virtue; and to disparage an art one has attempted to practise since the age of seven cannot but seem a gesture wholly theatrical. What honest craftsman, regardless alike of the appraisal of critics and the indulgence of readers, would squander a lifetime upon work that did not contain for him a certain measure of achievement?

If I were to deny my life as a writer, it would mean the denial of all that to me has represented reality. Like every other wilful author, I have led, for as many years as I can remember, a dual existence. The natural writer must, of necessity, live on the surface the life of accepted facts, which is the life of action and shadows, while with his deeper consciousness he continues to live that strangely valid life of the mind, which is related to the essence of things in themselves and to the more vivid world of the imagination. For these reasons, if for none other, I shall remark, without excuse, that just as the dullest autobiography may count upon one attentive and interested reader, so the method of any persistent novelist is important to at least one writer.

E. G.

Novels of the Commonwealth

What the South needs is blood and irony. . . .

THE BATTLE-GROUND

"THE BATTLE-GROUND," published in 1902, is
the first of a series of novels which com-
poses, in the more freely interpretative form
of fiction, a social history of Virginia from the
decade before the Confederacy. *The Voice of the
People* was published two years before this story
appeared; but, in idea at least, both *The Battle-
Ground* and *The Deliverance* were already conceived; and it was while I waited to complete my
researches, and give them time to sink into my unconscious mind, that I wrote *The Voice of the
People* from an effortless and inherited knowledge.

Considered as history in the semblance of fiction, these six volumes would fall naturally into
the following chronological order:

I *The Battle-Ground* (1850-1865).
II *The Deliverance* (1878-1890).
III *The Voice of the People* (1870-1898).
IV *The Romance of a Plain Man* (1875-1910).
V *Virginia* (1884-1912).
VI *Life and Gabriella* (1894-1912).

To this series concerning the Commonwealth at large, I added, in later years and more mature work, two other groups, which comprise three novels of the country and four novels of the city. The country group includes:

The Miller of Old Church (1898-1902).
Barren Ground (1894-1924).
Vein of Iron (1901-1933).

The novels of the city embrace:

The Sheltered Life (1910-1917).
The Romantic Comedians (1923).
They Stooped to Folly (1924).
In This Our Life (1938-1939).

Such, then, is the completed design which had its beginning in the first decade of the twentieth century. While American fiction entertained itself with an historical pageant, I began a history of manners that would embrace those aspects of Southern life with which I was acquainted. I intended to treat the static customs of the country, as well as the changing provincial fashions of the small towns and cities. Moreover, I planned to portray the different social orders, and especially, for this would constitute the major theme of my chronicle, the rise of the middle class as the dominant force in Southern democracy. From the year 1899 until the beginning of the First World War, I was at work on this series. By the time the war had ended, however, I felt that I had finished with history, and that I was now able to break fresh ground, and at least to lay the foundations of a more permanent structure. In my own critical opinion, my best books have been written since 1922; yet all these later novels, from *Barren Ground* to *In This Our Life,* were so arranged as to fall within the now broadened scope of my original plan.

Although *The Battle-Ground* is not a romance, it is, nevertheless, the work of romantic youth. The person who conceived it is, nowadays, a dead person. I cannot put myself in the place of the author. I cannot summon back that long-departed spirit and assign it to a name and a body. But the book still stands for what it was in my early youth; and it appears to keep its hold on another youth in another moment of history. Throughout the years, it has not lost a loyal company of well-wishers, in the face of the ever-changing fashions of literature. With the possible exception of Dorinda Oakley in *Barren Ground,* Betty Ambler has been the best liked of my heroines, as the leading women characters in fiction used to be called. For the South at least, she seemed to personify the spirit that fought with gallantry and gaiety, and that in defeat remained undefeated.

Because the work was finished, and I could not write it over, I did not attempt to revise it fundamentally. Sentences here and there I have altered from the original version; but in the book as a whole I could find no obvious error either of fact or of atmosphere. Since I wrote *The Battle-Ground,* I have read, it is true, a history of fashions. I have learned the exact date that marked the widening of crinolines; and I have learned, also, the year in which the black stock yielded place to the cravat, and the still later year in which Dan returned from Paris with the news that neckties were coming in and large cravats were beginning to go out. But, for all my close scrutiny, I could detect no flaw in the verisimilitude of the picture.

From time to time, at longer intervals, this novel approaches me in a new dress from a new direction; and only this morning, I received a copy of a neat edition in red, which is designed for the use of schools and colleges. So it passes farther and farther away, until the remote face it turns backward has become the face of a stranger. I fail to recognize any feature; I feel not the slightest bond of human or literary relationship. And I find it pensively amusing to recall that, while I was writing *The Battle-Ground,* I imagined that only the old, or at least the elderly, who could appreciate its accuracy, would enjoy this evocation of a lost way of living.

It may be true that one's dead youth must always appear unfamiliar when one looks back on it through the changing years. Probably, if not certainly, these early novels, which now seem to me so deficient in worldly wisdom and in the sense of experience, are more faithful to the reality of their time and place than I could, in the present, hope to make any record of that obliterated epoch. And since it has been decreed that every work of man, as well as man himself, must sooner or later become "dated," it is consoling to remember that, provided the reversed view is long enough, all dates come at last to look alike in the indifferent pages of history. But almost any position is safer, one surmises, than that of the unhappy anachronism.

I had read, to be sure, a vast amount of writing, and the major part of this writing had happened, by accident, to be literature. Yet when I began to write novels, I had not, so far as I can recall, read any literature that discussed the making of literature. I knew a little of Aristotle; and from him, I had imperfectly derived a few working principles of self-criticism. But I was unfamiliar with the modern analytical methods; and, if we except the work of the English essayists, I was ignorant of the whole new world of theories waiting, just beyond my outlook, to be discovered and explored.

This discovery was to come to me afterwards; for, just as a child must learn to talk and to walk naturally, so even the instinctive writer must acquire the simple first principles of his craft. I had hoped to find an easier way. But by the time I had discovered these less ancient theories, I had discovered also that there is in writing no easier way anywhere, and that there is, indeed, no single easy step in the practice of this difficult art.

For the rest, though I had not read Wordsworth's great *Preface to Lyrical Ballads,* or, in fact, any of the "new" criticism, which was already so old, I was, in my humble place and way, beginning a solitary revolt against the formal, the false, the affected, the sentimental, and the pretentious, in Southern writing. I had no guide. I was, so far as I was then aware, alone in my rejection of a prescribed and moribund convention of letters. But I felt, "Life is not like this." I thought, "Why must novels be false to experience?" No hint of an outside revolution in ideas had ever penetrated the walls of our library. Only life had broken through those elegiac tones which were still the common chord in all Southern prose fiction. And as life broke into the surrounding gloom, I felt that I could not thrive or even breathe, as a novelist, in a funereal air. Yet how could I escape? So urgent was my need that, in my first story, I had gone too far in the opposite way, and that story had been, from my point of view, merely a youthful failure. In a recoil from the uniform Southern heroes in fiction, I had taken as my central figure one of the despised and rejected of society, an illegitimate offspring of the peasant or "poor white" class. "But it is incredible," declared one of my elderly kinsmen, in the face of all English literature, to say nothing of Abraham, "that a well-brought-up Southern girl should even know what a bastard is."

The Descendant, my first published book, which I had begun at eighteen and had put aside for several years before it was remembered and finished, had seen the light for a brief hour and been thrust back into oblivion. Even the effort to find a publisher appeared to me to have been wasted. The trouble, I can now see, was that I had come twenty years, or nearer thirty years, before the period in which I might have found myself welcome. In the year 1897, I was writing in the mood, and with something of the manner, or the lack of manner, I regret to say, of the present decade. Nowadays, American novels are filled with illegitimate offspring, and New York is over-crowded with vociferous young radicals, just escaped from the South; but in the eighteen-nineties, my sullen Socialist encountered only the fear and suspicion that the unfamiliar inspires. It was an era when people, not only respected the genteel tradition, but even enjoyed reading about it. After forty years, I am able to recall with some amusement, that *The Descendant* was mildly praised or censured by William Dean Howells, because of its "intensity" —or was it "vitality"?—whereas, in another, though less eminent, quarter the harmless little work was attacked, not without violence, alike because it quoted "the philosopher Schopenhauer, who was wanting both in reverence for God and chivalry to women," and because it bore upon its title page "the impious assertion, attributed to Haeckel, that man is not above nature, but in nature."

So it seemed to me, in 1897, that I did not belong in the South, that I did not belong in the North, that I did not belong in any place or period I had so far discovered. In New York, all that I could strive for would be Cézanne's "little sensation" in art, and I had even less ambition to provide "the little sensation" in my work than I had the need to display it in my own person. But I was excited by the wish to express an idea that troubled my consciousness. I was worried by the knowledge that I had attained as yet no appropriate vehicle for that expression.

In looking back over the years, I have often wondered whether any other obstinate author could ever have received so little understanding encouragement. Of encouragement that was misunderstanding, I had, I think, a little more than my share. Twenty-five years later, in a review of *Barren Ground,* Stuart P. Sherman remarked, "Northern critics have never known how to take her": but, at the turn of the century, there were no visible Southern critics; and had there been, they would have repudiated any novelist who had attempted to pierce, or even to prick, the sentimental fallacy. In Southern fiction there were many romances of the Confederacy; but so far as I am aware, they had, one and all, followed faithfully a well-worn and standardized pattern. A gallant Northern invader (though never of the rank and file) must rescue the person and protect the virtue of a spirited yet clinging Southern belle and beauty. Every Christmas, after I had passed into my second reader, I had received one of these perennial romances, usually in a cheaper reprint (since books have always been regarded by Southerners as the last of the luxuries), and each annual appearance, neatly inscribed in the fine Italian penmanship of a maiden aunt, had added fuel to a slowly kindling fire of revolt. I could not believe that war was like that. I had never been young enough to believe it. I could not believe that the late invasion had been a romantic conflict between handsome soldiers in blue uniforms and Southern ladies in crinolines.

Although I was not born until the middle of the eighteen-seventies, I could well remember the hungry 'eighties; and I could remember, too, that when I wanted a doll with "real hair," I was told I could not have it because we had "lost everything in the war." A war in which one had lost everything, even the right to own a doll with real hair, was not precisely my idea of a romance. All I knew of the Civil War was what I had heard from my mother, supported by a chanting chorus of male and female voices. There was, in particular, a grand-aunt of lugubrious bearing, as unlike the Southern belle in fiction as one could imagine; and I never think of her without recalling a speckled engraving of Hecuba Lamenting over the Ruins of Troy. It was not that I disliked legend. On the contrary, I still believe that a heroic legend is the noblest creation of man. But I believe also that legend to be a blessing must be re-created not in funeral wreaths, but in dynamic tradition, and in the living character of a race. I had grown up in the yet lingering fragrance of the old South; and I loved its imperishable charm, even while I revolted from its stranglehold on the intellect. Like the new South, I had inherited the tragic conflict of types.

In *The Battle-Ground,* I have tried to portray the last stand in Virginia of the aristocratic tradition. Whether this tradition was an imported English product or a native flower of the country, is a question of no particular moment. Any faith that moulds and influences the plastic character of a people has validity for those who live under it and believe in it. The culture it creates and establishes is a reality so long as it survives. In the old South, this inherited culture possessed grace and beauty and the inspiration of gaiety. Yet it was shallow-rooted at best, since, for all its charm and its good will, the way of living depended, not upon its own creative strength, but upon the enforced servitude of an alien race. Not the fortunes of war, not the moral order of the universe, but economic necessity doomed the South to defeat. In the coming industrial conquest, the aristocratic tradition could survive only as an archaic memorial. It was condemned to stand alone because it had been forsaken by time.

Before writing this book, which was designed to begin a history of the social transition by imaginatively restoring the old order, I visited every scene in my narrative, and studied every angle of vision. My material was well in hand; but I was groping my youthful way toward an adequate method, which must be, at the same time, a method that was wholly unconscious, that had been, as it were, organized into an instinct. Although, as I have indicated, I was ignorant of literary theories, I was, nevertheless, ripe for the invigorating influence of the first great realistic novelists, whose books were then only beginning to be widely read in America. The American school of refined realism, which had flourished chiefly in New England, had not, at that time, surrendered the seat of authority to the brawny vigour of the Middle West. Mr. Howells was still the acting dean of a severely regimented American realism. And all my life I had been a rebel against regimentation in any form. I had not revolted from the Southern sentimental fallacy in order to submit myself to the tyranny of the Northern genteel tradition. The true realists, I felt, must illuminate experience, not merely transcribe it; and so, for my own purpose, I defined the art of fiction as experience illuminated.

One of the few intellectual advantages of my youth was the faculty with which I discovered ideas, through some sympathetic attraction, at the moment I needed them. Since I have never approached literature by way of college courses in English, arranged neatly with dates of birth and death in a lank row of epitaphs, books have been, for me, one of the vital elements of experience, not a thing apart, not a collection of classified facts. Great novels, as I have come upon them, either in youth or in later years, have unerringly revealed the human mind and heart as these are affected or controlled by the deeper realities. Always there has been illumination, and always this illumination has fallen straight on the subject. I cared nothing for labels. What I wanted was an interpretation of life. Whether the vehicle was termed romance or realism seemed unimportant, if only the novel contained the breath of life and had been rounded out by its own organism. My quarrel, alike with Southern romance and Northern realism, was simply the old resentment against fixed patterns of work and the rule of averages in general. At the moment, in the long and now slowly fading dawn of realism as a revolutionary idea, I felt myself to be a realist in the making at least. Years afterwards, when the post-war disintegration had crowded the Southern landscape with seekers of "the little sensation," and when realism had so often degenerated into literary ruffianism, I found that I was once again a rebel in letters. For I was in search of truth, not sensation; and I began to suspect that I was as little likely to encounter truth in the exposed features of the new barbarism as under the mask of civilized conduct. Although I was not unwilling to admit, granted the burden of proof, that life on a globe which has been called the meanest of the planets may be merely an excrescence of aging matter, and the whole human breed a spawn of glorified maggots, I still failed to see the necessity either of embalming maggots in literature or of keeping them alive on relief.

But in the year 1900, all these problems, with many others, belonged to the future. In the immediate present, we could discern nothing more threatening to the moral order than a babel of costume romances and a literary epidemic of curled wigs and lace ruffles.

It is true that I had read little of Tolstoy, and nothing at all of Turgenev, Chekhov, and Dostoevsky. But I had read Balzac; I had read Flaubert; I had read Maupassant; I had read every celebrated novel written in English. And I had not read them wholly in vain. They had taught me that the external truth of the subject must depend upon the absolute fidelity of the treatment, and that the chief, the supreme merit lies in the vision of the artist, in the direct light of imagination. For the first time, I perceived with clearness what I had always felt vaguely, that the assembling of material, the arrangement of masses, may have greater effect than the material itself. A wrong slant of light, a false point of view, a person or

object out of focus, a slight failure in perspective
—a single one of these errors may drain the life
and colour from any landscape, from any figure.
Taken together, they may turn natural movement
into a sluggish or a delirious pace; they may change
living and animated features into a literary death-
mask. And just as the wrong handling or lighting
may extinguish vitality, so the right arrangement
of parts may bring out latent and unsuspected possibilities in the simplest scene or situation.

From those explorers of the heart, the true realists, I learned also, if I had not already perceived
this elementary principle in the canons of art, that
a universe of ideas divides the novel bearing a sin-
cere emotion toward life from the novel that depends upon a sterile convention. All this, as a
youthful author, I owed to the theory of realism
in fiction, and to the fighting strength I derived
from that theory. I can still remember the glow
enkindled in my imagination by Maupassant's
story of the two quite ordinary men who went out
for a day's quiet fishing during the Franco-Prus-
sian War, only to discover that they were not ordinary men but heroes. This was literary realism, as
I understood and accepted the name. It meant the
way of the swift stroke, of the clean cut, of the
deep penetration into experience.

As I glance back over the first decade of the

twentieth century, the period stands out, in America at least, as a time of literary imitation. So far, I had never met a novelist, or indeed any other sort of writer, in the flesh; and the whole profession existed for me as a tribe slightly fabulous. Yet a more or less literary journal would sometimes drift my way; and from this authoritative source, I gathered that all successful novelists, except the few brave young men who frolicked after the sunflower or the green carnation, were engaged in "doing a Henry James novel." Well, I admired Henry James; I even enjoyed his books, which so few of his admirers appeared to do; but I felt not the slightest disposition to imitate him or any one else. And, even if I had found no better reason, I should soon have discovered that there was not room enough for me in that over-crowded literary life-boat.

I cannot recall when I first comprehended the importance, in novel writing, of the author's total immersion. It may be that I was born with that understanding. Certainly I had never felt an inclination to thrust myself into the situation, though many of my favourite novelists took the liberty of slipping in and out of their books as easily as a jack-in-the-box. The major obligation of adhering to a single, or at least a restricted, point of view came to me more gradually. In *The Battle-*

Ground, the subject is surveyed, not only through the eyes of the two central figures, but, on several occasions, it is recorded in the minds of less prominent characters. Moreover, although not ever appearing in person, a narrator remains permanently in the background, even when unobserved, and directs the flow of pure narrative. My strength in this early writing was not equal to the single curve I follow in *Barren Ground.* The mind of Dorinda is the theatre for that later drama; and nothing enters the scope of the novel which might not have fallen within range of her experience or imagination. All that the author, or the reader, knows of the situation is what it has meant to Dorinda, either through her own consciousness, or through the impressions which persons or objects have left upon her. In *The Battle-Ground,* the point of view is more variable, and the curve of approach remains less direct.

What I tried to do in *The Battle-Ground* was to write, not literally a novel of war, but a chronicle of two neighbouring families, the Amblers and the Lightfoots, who had lived through a disastrous period in history. If I used the Civil War as a background, it was merely as one of several circumstances which had moulded the character of the individual Virginian, as well as the social order in which he made a vital, if obscure, figure. There was, I knew, rich and deep material under the transparent legends of the South. The adventures of my mother, as a young wife during the war, were as vivid to me as my own memories; and many of the minor characters in the book were sketched from her description of living figures. It is true that I had seen none of these people in the flesh; but even if the Major and Mrs. Lightfoot and Miss Lydia and Big Abel appeared to me in imagination only, they were, each and all, in an exact and literal sense, real persons.

Major Lightfoot was a kinsman of my father. At the beginning of the war, he was an elderly statesman, and, like many other elderly statesmen, a violent non-combatant. His beautiful old home was burned in an invasion of the Valley; but the name of the place was not Chericoke. Instead of using his wife as a model for Mrs. Lightfoot, I drew that woman of infinite resources from a great-grand-aunt on the distaff side of the family. As a little child, my mother had often seen this old lady reading *The Mysteries of Udolpho,* in her tester bed, by the light of a candle in a tall silver candlestick, which Mitty, her small coloured maid, snuffed whenever the wick needed attention, or extinguished entirely as soon as her mistress showed signs of falling asleep.

Over and over again, I had fought the battles of

that war, or marched to Appomattox with survivors of the ragged army. While I was writing this
book, I had in my possession complete files, from
1860 to 1865, of *The Richmond Enquirer, The
Richmond Examiner,* and *The New York Herald.*
Yet what I recall most vividly is spring and summer in the Valley of Virginia, when I went over
the scene and outlined my story. It is true that I had
read innumerable diaries and letters; but I have
not the kind of mind that multiplies figures and assembles masses of data; and for my novel, tinged
as it is with the colours of an ornamental age, I
depended chiefly upon the incidents I had gathered from actual participants. Always I was col-
lecting impressions, rather than facts, for the first
three volumes in my proposed social history. And
since I was still in my middle twenties, it was inevitable, no doubt, that these volumes should reflect a romantic idealism. With my next two books,
the idealism began to be flavoured with irony,
until gradually, or so it seemed to me, I escaped
entirely from the undue influence of ancestor worship. Yet this realistic vision of the universe and
our humble part in it does not necessarily disavow
the quality of romance, which, as long as it survives in our little life, will continue to create the
belief in its own permanence.

Nothing in my inquiries into the past had in-

terested me more than the democratic feeling in
the Army of Northern Virginia. Here, in the rank
and file, men who considered themselves aristocrats marched on a level with men who did not
care whether or not they were plebeians. Superficial gradations were submerged in a universal
emotion. Up from the Tidewater with Lee, or
down from the mountains with Stonewall Jackson,
these men trooped, separately or together, as Virginians eager to defend their soil from an invader.
In "Pinetop," who had hastened down from his
mountain cabin to follow "Old Stonewall," I have
tried to render a tragedy within a tragedy. Here
was a Southerner who had never owned a slave,
and rarely seen one, offering his life in defense,
not only of an abstract right, which meant nothing
to him, but also of institutions which bore more
hardly upon the illiterate white man than they
bore upon the black man in chattel slavery. Mont-
joy, who owned Big Abel, and "Pinetop," who
had never owned anything, not even a knowledge
of the alphabet, formed a close comradeship in the
Army of Northern Virginia. Throughout the
course of history, such instances are not uncommon; and we find, again and again, that men will
fight desperately, provided an emotion or an instinct responds, to perpetuate systems and institutions which will work only to destroy their de-

fenders. My idea in dramatizing this special incident was to invest one of the eternal paradoxes of human nature with a visible form.

It is the fashion nowadays to subordinate art to utility, and philosophy to invention, at the very moment in which we are elevating emotion above reason and instinct beyond intellect. But the uncertain mechanism of the human mind, universal or individual, possesses, fortunately for us, the merits of its defects. Even in the stream of consciousness there is a tide which must inevitably turn at the flood. "When reason is against a man," said Hume, "he will soon turn against reason"; and the remark is not less applicable to an age than to a man. Nevertheless, I imagine, the world's hope must lie in the thought that reason may turn also. Once again, if only we can arrange to live long enough, the arts may rise above what we call "the utilities," philosophy may yet, in some crisis of the eternal recurrence, triumph over invention, and the intellect may outlast the recent assault on intellectualism along the popular front. In the accommodating processes of evolution, while nature is scrupulously looking after large matters and organic forms of life, even so small a body as the novel may not miss entirely the effects of this perpetual rhythm and change. The history of fiction

23

might serve, indeed, as a not unworthy companion volume to the history of man's changing views of himself and the universe.

From its rudimentary outlines and embryonic flutters in a firelit cave, the art of fiction has remained the most accurate mirror of the different stages in the pilgrimage of humanity. Centuries before Richardson, the primitive story-teller and his successors had depicted, however fumblingly, both emotion and instinct. And as I comprehended this, I comprehended even more clearly that, though the chief end of the novel is to create life, there is a secondary obligation which demands that fiction shall, in a measure at least, reflect the movement and the tone of its age. This, to be definite, is the purpose I have tried to serve in this undocumented chronicle of human nature and the conditions under which it developed, or by which it was modified, in related periods of time. Although I feel that the representation is wholly inadequate, I am compelled to leave it as it is, because the ambitious author has long since passed away.

And so, once again, I must repeat myself. If I have dealt with the spirit of romance, it is because one cannot approach the Confederacy without touching the very heart of romantic tradition. It is the single occasion in American history, and one of the rare occasions in the history of the world, when the conflict of actualities was profoundly romantic. For Virginia, in that disastrous illusion, the Confederacy was the expiring gesture of chivalry.

THE DELIVERANCE

LIKE many of my other novels, *The Deliver-ance* flowered from a seed dropped care-lessly in my mind when I was a child. The story of Mrs. Blake (or at least the original inci-dent, for in *The Deliverance* this story was altered almost beyond recognition) was related to me, with many details, by a romantic elderly lady of my acquaintance.

At the time, I could not have been more than nine or ten years of age; but I can still see the long dim drawing-room sheltered from the world by Brussels lace curtains. I can see the faded Colonial wall paper, with its pattern of yellow ships and blue water, the elaborate wire cage containing an ancient parrot that had lost part of his handsome red and green plumage, and the large, calm, slightly mottled, and invincibly smiling, features of the romantic lady, who had short, very curly grey hair, and wore in the lace at her throat a cameo brooch bearing the head of Athena. Many years afterwards, this treasured friend of my childhood lived again for me as Miss Priscilla Batte in *Virginia*.

While I brooded over my intended series of novels, this occasion flickered back to life in my memory. Gradually, after the habit of ideas that have lain long buried beneath clustering impressions, the image of Mrs. Blake gathered symbolic substance and power. I saw in her, not one old woman groping, blind and nourished by illusions, through a memorable epoch in history, but Virginia and the entire South, unaware of the changes about them, clinging, with passionate fidelity, to the ceremonial forms of tradition.

In looking back on *The Deliverance* after thirty-four years, I can but realize that the theme was not completely developed. The book was written too soon. I grew slowly; I matured late; and my earliest novels were the result of intuitive understanding alone. In theory, I am convinced that one cannot become a novelist of character until one has lived for at least thirty—or, better still, forty years. It is not sufficient to test life; one should consume and assimilate it before one attempts to cast fresh experience into a permanent form. For the pure romancer, intuition may be all that is necessary, especially when, as with Emily Brontë, it is the intuition of genius. But I was never a pure romancer any more than I was a pure realist.

27

Rather I should have called myself a verist had such a term come my way. The whole truth must embrace the interior world as well as external appearances. Behaviour alone is only the outer envelope of personality; and this is why documentary realism, the notebook style, has produced merely surface impressions. Whenever it has achieved true greatness, as we find in the work of Flaubert, for example, it is because genius instinctively rejects every formula, including its own, and the art of fiction has triumphed over and absorbed the nature of facts. When all is said, the arteries in the intellect are as essential to literature as the arteries in the body are essential to life. Of this I was thinking many years ago when I said that the South needed blood and irony. Blood it needed because Southern culture had strained too far away from its roots in the earth; it had grown thin and pale; it was satisfied to exist on borrowed ideas, to copy instead of create. And irony is an indispensable ingredient of the critical vision; it is the safest antidote to sentimental decay.

But, in the beginning, I was impatient to rush ahead into print, when I should have been content to grow slowly, after my fashion, from roots which were deep and strong, and nourished by both the poetry and prose of tradition. Instead of shooting up quickly into the light and air, the seeds

of this book should have remained for a longer
period of time, undisturbed, where they had fallen
in my imagination. The incident I remembered
was not vigorous enough to sustain the full
strength of the climax. Had I waited, the book
might have been better; on the other hand, it
might never have been written at all. Be that as it
may, the design of the structure, if one consents
to overlook a certain natural exuberance, still appears to be sufficiently logical. The movement
runs consistently through the chain of occurrences;
and the theme springs, as the themes of so many
novels of the soil have done, from some intrinsic
values of the time and place.

In outlining *The Deliverance,* my purpose was
to interpret with fidelity, not spectacular events or
dramatic moments, but the prolonged effects of
the social transition upon ordinary lives that were
lived by simple folk, alike in the defeated aristocracy and the intransigent democracy. Colonial
pieces in fiction were then popular, and the literary woods were filled with stalking savages and
captive damsels in fancy dress. "You must write
historical romances if you wish to be popular," in-
sisted my sagacious publisher, who had recently
induced Miss Mary E. Wilkins to perpetrate a
romance of Colonial Virginia. But popularity,
though agreeable no doubt, was not, as I vainly

tried to convince him, the ultimate standard. There are others, though one might be hard put to it in naming them over. That I should ever become a popular writer, indeed, had never occurred to me. I knew too well that, for such an end, I had taken the wrong turn and was still moving steadily in the wrong direction. Long before, I had learned, without knowing when or where, that to be honest and yet popular is almost as difficult in literature as it is in life.

The chief end of the novel, as indeed of all literature, I felt, was to increase our understanding of life and heighten our consciousness. To do this, writing must not only render experience, it must interpret and intensify the daily processes of living. I saw a fertile, an almost virgin, field ahead of me, and I knew that I lacked only the necessary art to make it yield a rich harvest. The soil was deep and dark with a thick deposit of unused material, for it appeared that the romancers of that golden age were merely scratching the surface. I felt that farther down there was a vital warmth, the warmth of humble lives that have been lived near the earth; but I was deficient, I perceived, after my first effort, in the proper tools for experiment. The substance was all there; and when I speak, as I have done elsewhere, of the oldest roots in our Republic, I mean, of course, the oldest roots of democracy. However far and deep Spanish roots may have penetrated, they did not spring up again to flower in American institutions.

In this novel, as in *Barren Ground,* I have tried to depict the land as a living personality, and to portray its characteristics in the central figures. There is in every human being, I think, a native country of the mind, where, protected by inaccessible barriers, the sensitive dream life may exist safely. Frequently, the fields within are no more than an extension of some lost and remembered earlier surroundings. However that may be, my country of the mind was, for the purposes of fiction at least, the familiar Virginian scene of my childhood. My happiest days were those in which I ran wild over the red clay roads and the ragged fields, where the shadows of birds flitted by, and a secret community of small furry creatures scurried close to the ground.

But I needed more than a landscape, however human its moods and its features. I needed a genuine growth from the soil, a natural abundance; and, for this reason no doubt, I placed my story among the tobacco fields, in that part of Virginia where tobacco possesses an almost elemental power to bless or to curse. Yet I cannot recall that I deliberately selected this country. When I first saw Christopher Blake, he was moving in the centre of a ploughed field, just as Mr. Carraway, the lawyer, found him, while he dropped the young tobacco plants into the earth. Immediately I knew that this was his appropriate setting, and I never thought of him afterwards as detached from that background.

As a child I had been familiar with the uncertain crop of tobacco; and I had followed the different stages of growth, from the first seedlings to the curing of the luxuriant leaves. No sooner had I recognized the right surroundings for my narrative than I decided to go back to the farm and retrace the entire scene by the side of a tenant farmer. Together, we moved up and down through the long furrows; and with the changing seasons, we dropped young plants into the earth, or watched the "suckers" pinched off as the stalks shot up in the hot sunshine. For a month or more, scarcely longer, the whole landscape would be clothed with wave after wave of a rich tropical green, which was gradually tinged with yellow as the immense leaves matured. Methods have changed, even in Virginia, in the past thirty-four years; but when *The Deliverance* was first published, many readers remarked that the pages were "drenched with the smell of tobacco."

What I had in mind, as I have said, was to construct a scene in which the human figures would appear as natural projections of the landscape. For this purpose, I felt that I must avoid the middle shades and work in two strongly contrasting tones of light and darkness. And I felt also that both the central character and the background must be composed of these light and dark contrasts. In my other books, especially in my later comedies of manners, I have preferred to use more subtle gradations of approach; but for this special narrative, I knew that all the impressions of the scene should be as primitive as the mind and heart of my leading figure, which were controlled by violence, and by the elemental motives of desire and revenge. Between Christopher and his environment there must be an unbroken sympathetic accord; for, denied all inner harmony, he could find peace and freedom only in communion with that earth which had moulded both him and his race. And so, hatred, not love, would be the dominant theme of this record of lives defending a lost heritage. The tone would be harsh, and the illumination would never be softened or diffused. Inwardly, the light of introspection must fall on the troubled soul of Christopher Blake, while without, the light of day flashed from a sky which was, at intervals, dark or sullen. For this story, as I wove the outline with my inadequate youthful technique, was meant to

33

follow an epic curve and to be bathed in an epic quality of atmosphere.

In the character of Christopher Blake, I was trying to test the strength of hereditary fibre when it has been long subjected to the power of malignant circumstances. My own theory had inclined to the belief that environment more than inheritance determines character. What it does not determine is the tendency of native impulse nurtured by tradition and legend, unless tradition and legend may be considered a part of environment. Had I been older and possessed of a wider experience, I should have left out, or at least subordinated, the part that romantic love plays in the triumph over revenge. The book would have been stronger, I think, if I had narrowed down the range of the theme, and held it firmly to the bare anatomy of inherited hatred. Certainly the novel would have gained firmness of structure by this logical simplification.

Even so, I have never ceased to regret that Christopher Blake fell so far short of the figure that lived in my image-making faculty. Outwardly, at least, he resembled a man whom I had known as a very young girl. There was the remembered heroic stature, the wheat-coloured hair bound by an invisible garland, the frowning storm-clouded gaze—well, in brief, there was the changeless outline of youth and of legend. But the portrait went no deeper than superficial appearance. For the rest, Christopher was the embodiment of a period in violent transition; and in this transition, the dark tumult of war had been cast up from the torn earth and had entered the open mind of a child. Hatred was not of the will alone; it had been absorbed into his blood, and was inextricably woven through every nerve of his body. One might tear it out only by plucking up the secret roots of his identity.

If Christopher embodied time in convulsion, the subsidiary characters represented the long upheaval of a social order. After the confusion and the vindictive ingenuity of the Reconstruction Acts, the stifled resentment of the defeated lingered on far into the future. It was an epoch of crisis, of spiritual and physical sickness, of smouldering antagonisms under the surface of life. Men's minds were darkened or inflamed by recent paroxysms of fear; and both fear and faith clung with passion to the few surviving semblances of stability. In this mood, the past became not only cherished but sanctified; and the dream world of Mrs. Blake appeared more as a general state of mind than as the fantasy of a nostalgic old woman. She personified the lost illusions of the Southern heart; and it is not without significance that the woman in my drama should have had her tragic prototype in the flesh. Her probability has been questioned, but without, I think, an understanding of the actual conditions. So profound had been her former sense of security and permanence, so unreasoning her belief in a personal Providence, and her veneration for religious and social taboos, so invulnerable her pride of name and estate, that even had her eyes been suddenly opened, in all likelihood she would have looked on her fallen fortunes merely as a sort of inopportune masquerade. When her children exalted her into an idol of sacrifice, each member was conforming to the authentic spirit and manner of a past way of living. In the Virginia of that not too distant day, and indeed in the world beyond the borders of the Commonwealth, thousands of daughters were slowly dragging out a family martyrdom without faith. In the love of Lila Blake and Jim Weatherby, there is a more sanguine union of opposites; and this also was a natural result of the changing orders. For several of my Negro characters, I went directly to life; for I was writing of a region where servants had always been plentiful, and where the slaves of the tobacco planters had formed an essential part of the social system. That aspect, it is needless to relate, is as dead nowadays as the customs of Nineveh. Yet, even in my childhood, such servants were not uncommon, and I have tried to render them faithfully.

In Fletcher, the upstart, I have treated the darkest side of transition. For a brighter picture, one may turn to *The Voice of the People* and *The Romance of a Plain Man,* parallel studies of the rise of the working class. But society in convulsion will cast up a sinister spawn; and Fletcher's breed is all too numerous in the sullen years which must follow invasion and conquest on any part of the globe. It is probable, however, that the Southern variation of his type will never be analyzed. Was he simply what used to be called, with unsentimental accuracy, "a bad lot"? Or was he the victim of prolonged social injustice and the functional derangement of civilization? There is evidence that his kind still persists even in an age of milder beliefs and more liberal behaviour. For his sins, to use a term he would have respected, were rooted in the two oldest and deepest instincts in human nature, cruelty and greed.

Because this was to be a book of strong contradictions, I found myself, without intentional design, distributing the action and incidents in a way that would emphasize the uses of contrast. The theme was charged, I felt, with dramatic possibilities; but so far as my equipment permitted, I tried to avoid the too obvious pitfalls of melodrama, and to paint an accurate picture of the place and the period. Though I have called my novel a romance, my youthful realistic vision would not allow me to over-romanticize my material. On the contrary, it was exactly this element of romance in any true realism that I was trying more to subdue than to emphasize. The theme, as well as the background, was instinct with romantic quality, not only in my narrative, but equally in the actual living scene and in the original model of Christopher Blake. Scrupulously as I toned down the delineation, it retained, nevertheless, the outward semblance of romance, though it was still, and I found comfort in this reflection, a romance with its feet on the ground. The vital framework, once called a plot, was of that animated nature which required a firm hand to prevent its breaking out into sensational movement. I was dealing with the simple passions of the heart, and, without urging or direction, they would create for themselves the raw substance of drama.

Against this background of dissolution, the figures of Tucker and Aunt Saidie represent normal, if not average, persons, who, amid general anarchy, are still able to look disaster out of countenance. Aunt Saidie was merely an ignorant woman of good nature, but Tucker was a civilized soul in a world which, by and large, is not, and may not ever become, civilized. His true companions in my books are General Archbald in *The Sheltered Life* and John Fincastle in *Vein of Iron*. This rare pattern of mankind has always attracted me as a novelist. I like to imagine how the world would appear if human beings were really civilized, not by machinery alone, but through that nobler organ which has been called, the heart in the intellect. My portrait of Tucker shows an immature grasp of my subject; and he is not entirely free from the quixotic idealism which clashed with decadent sensationalism at the end of the century. Yet his crutch also was firmly planted on the common ground; and this is as much perhaps as one has the right to expect from any romantic philosopher.

In the character of Maria Fletcher, I have dealt again with the higher offspring of a lower form. Just as Nicholas Burr in *The Voice of the People* was a superior variation from an inferior type, so Maria exemplified a woman's upspringing from poorer stock, and her development away from the family pattern. Her emergence, however, would fail to serve as a test, because she had inherited a better strain from her mother, and this single strain may have helped to defeat the centripetal forces of long inbreeding. Against her triumph, one may place the failure of the boy Will, a weakling of arrested moral development, who had been subjected, with Maria, to the worst influences of both heredity and training. And even Maria needed the severe discipline of unhappiness, as well as the enlightenment of passion, to reveal the finer grain of her nature. The love of Christopher and Maria, as I tried to present it in fiction, sprang, not only from that strange attraction which appears sometimes to reside in hostile elements, but also from one of those sudden romantic fires which occasionally inflame and consume the arid substance of the actuality.

So my landscape was furnished, and my figures were clothed with the semblance of life. In this group, already so vital to me, I had hoped to render an epoch in history, while I moulded the theme and the train of events about a single centre of consciousness. My chief apprehension was that I might offend against the law of probability, which is the law of nature in all imaginary universes. It was not sufficient to separate my confused personalities from the general ferment. These detached fragments of a disordered world must mirror the scene about them in their destinies as human beings. For the first time, as I recall after thirty-four years, I encountered in this book the problem of direct or indirect approach to my subject. Until I began to plan *The Deliver-*

ance, questions of technique had seldom disturbed me; and I had written, without effort, from some deep instinct, which assured me that the way I saw was the one and only way of handling my theme. I had not paused to examine my method simply because I had not ever been aware of possessing a method. It is true that I had brooded long over my novels; but this intuitive process was divorced from the sober faculty of reason, and resembled rather the aimless musing of reverie. Instinct alone had warned me that a narrative should adhere to the central figure, and that looseness of structure, as well as thinning substance, was the result of a too variable field of vision.

But with *The Deliverance,* I found almost immediately that my novel needed an avenue of approach through a mind that was distinct from the mind of the author. It was imperative that one should first see Christopher Blake as he appeared to the eyes of a stranger; and it was for this purpose that I introduced Carraway, the attorney. In a measure, this perplexed yet sympathetic understanding shields Christopher, not only from the reader but also from the narrator, who stands invisible at a little distance. The rutted roads winding among the tobacco fields, the heroic figure of young Christopher, whose ancestors had owned all the earth that they looked on, and the burly frame of Fletcher, the former overseer, who had defrauded the Blakes of their heritage—all these images are observed through the eyes and the mind of the bewildered spectator.

While I was at work on the theme, I was convinced that this way of approach provided a sense of security, and that it enabled me to create, little by little, a world which appeared to me to be credible. The whole chain of incidents, large or small, helped to link together the connecting pieces of framework. Even the loss of Mrs. Blake's yellow cat and the old Negro woman selling chickens to Fletcher, had their part, with the accumulation of episodes, in revealing latent motives in the persons I tried to portray. Through a multitude of suggestions and implications, I was preparing the scene for the major tragedy of frustrated revenge.

It is true that I have not ever again used this indirect approach, so heartily favoured by Henry James, yet it served me sufficiently well, or so I thought, in the present novel. Had I plunged immediately into the tormented consciousness of Christopher Blake, I should have been obliged to sacrifice much of the external verisimilitude. But by observing him first in high relief against the tobacco fields, I hoped to invest his outward form with solidity, before the narrator entered his mind and became immersed in his interior existence.

Instead of concentrating on this single subject in the early chapters, and reducing the minor persons to mere details in the setting, it seemed natural to let the medium of Carraway's reflections endow each figure with some portion of significance. Fletcher's family group at Blake Hall and the dispossessed Blake circle in the cottage of the overseer are thus introduced with equal detachment. Not until the whole scene, including persons and objects, was first outlined and then filled in with substance, was the hidden world of introspection explored.

My idea, even though I am not sure that I perceived this intention until my novel was well under way, and the movement sustained, was to sweep every incident and event, and every person and object, however important or unimportant, into the main current of action. That motive, I still think, was sound, although in places the delineation might have been more subtle, and the handling more competent. In my effort to cover, or at least account for, so long a continuance of events, I have had recourse to the devices of soliloquy and reflection. The story does not begin until some years after the Civil War; but I have contrived, by these recurring flashes of memory, to reassemble former occurrences, and to produce, I hope, an effect of unbroken duration.

Had I written this book at the present time, it is probable that I should have subdued the romantic note to an ending of stark tragedy. Maria used to be, and perhaps still is, one of the well-thought-of women in my novels. After Virginia, in the book of that name, she was the favourite, I recall, of Mary Johnston, and of other women belonging to the earlier generation. But her nobility, I may confess, has never entirely convinced me. Moreover, I have doubted, in later years, whether any love, however exalted, could have conquered the triumphant hatred in Christopher's heart and mind. But I wrote the book as it came to me. It ran its own course, and I could not have bent the drama aside from the inevitable sequence of cause and effect. No sooner had Carraway walked out of the scene than the writer's consciousness thrust itself into the identity of Christopher Blake, and I found myself, as the narrator, living in him and through him. The novel ended as I had always known that it must end, for the last line was implicit in the first paragraph; and in spite of the stiffening of my realistic purpose, my imagination could not have undone a series of actions and events which, from the beginning, had been so clearly perceived. But the nucleus of the design, the living kernel of matter, was contained in the mutual attraction and repulsion between Christopher Blake and Will Fletcher, and in the unassuaged thirst for revenge, which drew Christopher back again and again to the boy he had doomed to destruction.

Although I had known Mrs. Blake only in legend, I have taken few liberties with her portrait. The single obvious disparity is that the real woman lived but a short time in her changed surroundings, while Mrs. Blake survived for a number of years. This tampering with the actuality was one of my few compromises with dramatic necessity. Fantastic as the deluded old lady may appear in the present, in my childhood she would have been easily classified as a slightly individualized type. Even in that lately deceased era, the Southern belle and beauty was still a recognized ornament to society. As an emblem, she followed closely the mid-Victorian ideal, and though her sort was found everywhere in the Western world, it was in Virginia that she seemed to attain her finest and latest flowering. In my comedies of manners, she appears, with equal fidelity to the part, both as Mrs. Birdsong in *The Sheltered Life* and as Mrs. Dalrymple in *They Stooped to Folly*.

Even when I was very young, I liked to write of old people, because the old alone have finality. What is true of the young today may be false tomorrow. They are enveloped in emotion; and emotion as a state of being is fluent and evanescent. It is impossible for anyone, even for an interpreter of human psychology, to place the centre of experience in a perpetual flux. But the old not only *know,* they have *been.* They are settled in the kind of peace that dwells always in the heart of a storm. In this stillness, where life has been lived as a whole, it is easier for the true novelist to measure and divide and distribute the material of fiction. Nevertheless, I have not felt entirely satisfied with my treatment of Mrs. Blake. Both before and afterwards, I think, I have depicted old people with more success. Mrs. Lightfoot, in *The Battle-Ground,* is more natural and convincing, and so is her irascible husband, the Major. Certainly the two aging men, Judge Bassett and General Battle, in *The Voice of the People,* are closer, I feel, to the qualities and the defects of our nature. But in all my later books, I have liked particularly to deal with men and women who, though still vital within, have been brutally left behind by the years. For life, even the generally magnified life in fiction, is not the inalienable property of youth; and it is even possible that, upon occasions, the fact of being may rise superior to the act of doing, as a praiseworthy human achievement.

When *The Deliverance* was first published in 1904, it won immediately the sort of critical success that used to be described as "sensational." The general, though seldom the gentle, reader, I fear, appeared to take the novel to heart, perhaps because it was not unanimously commended by self-appointed censors of letters. Nowadays, when the whole mood seems to me to be over-romantic, it is amusing to recall that exactly thirty-four years ago, this novel was rhetorically denounced from pulpits because of the offending nature of its realism. And it is amusing also to reflect that those modern romancers, mistakenly labelled "Southern realists," who are enjoying the more profitable disfavour of the present, neither recognize nor appreciate the advantages of their position in time.

THE VOICE OF THE PEOPLE

ALTHOUGH *The Voice of the People* was the first of my Virginian novels to be published, it was arranged, chronologically, as the third volume of my social history of the Commonwealth. In the beginning, I had planned the two preceding novels, though the incident that formed the continuing theme of *The Deliverance* did not awaken in my memory until I had finished *The Battle-Ground* and was ready to deal with the protracted effects of the Reconstruction period.

I was then in my middle twenties, and I had already published two more or less successful failures. Nicholas Burr, in *The Voice of the People,* is the civilized offspring of the primitive figure in *The Descendant.* It is true that there may have been a decreasing vehemence in my own revolt from tradition; but all this was a part, no doubt, of the inescapable logic of time. My early excursion into strange places had taught me that literature, like life, must spring from roots, and that it must contain the vital principle of growth. When I wrote of Virginia, I was interpreting a province of mind and matter that I knew as intimately as I knew the fields of my own consciousness. For this reason my knowledge would be subdued, of necessity, to that strange amalgamation of fact and fantasy from which the novelist constructs his world and weaves his patterns of the actuality.

A contemporary critic, whose sun rose in the Middle West, and is now slowly westering in New York, has politely assigned my first books to "the Southern school of local colour." Like so many other literary estimates, however, this classification is both casual and inaccurate. On the contrary, my first immature novels were conceived and written in an impassioned revolt, not only from the school of local colour, but from the current Victorian tradition in letters, and, more especially, from the sentimental elegiac tone this tradition had assumed in Virginia. With a sense of adventure, I had broken away, in my first book, from provincial prejudices and inhibitions. In *The Descendant,* I had chosen, as I have explained elsewhere, to speak for the disinherited of society; but at the turn of the century the ragged shirt was yet to become a fashion in literature, and my bewildered revolutionist found few defenders among critics who were quite as genteel as novelists, and even more romantic at heart. Only when the ragged shirt was changed for the political coat of many colours was the wearer commended alike by reviewers and readers.

My problem, then, was a practical one from the beginning. I was not in search of a point of view. I knew where I stood, and when I glance back, it appears to me that I was born with a philosophy—or was it only a special feeling for life? At that time it seemed also, true or false, that I was born with the knowledge of good and evil, of joy and sorrow. Subjects flocked round me, thick as starlings. The world I had seen may not have been romantic, but it had been always animated, and occasionally exciting. Intellectual activity was, for me, an endless adventure. At twenty, I had even less patience than I have now, at sixty, with the coloured spectacles of evasive idealism. And then, as now, my arch-antagonist was inhumanity. Young as I was, I had looked on American life and letters of the eighteen-nineties, and I had felt, without knowing why, that both refused to envisage the actualities. "If you must write, do write of Southern ladies and gentlemen," urged my near and distant relatives, approving of decorum, but wisely suspicious of "local talent." But no. If I must write, I had resolved to "write differently." Although I had a proper regard for sentiment, especially for my own, I was already sick of sentimentality; and, by some singular twist of thought, sentiment in Southern fiction appeared invariably to degenerate into sentimentality. The true romance was my delight. I was a lover of Scott and Dumas; but I had no leaning toward romances of a past that had never existed.

As a beginning author, I was concerned neither with material, which was abundant, nor with a point of view, which my reason or my temperament had already selected. What troubled me was the lack of an adequate method. Although with my first books I had not been aware, as I have said, of this deficiency, the practice of fiction soon taught me that many heartburnings might be saved by knowing not only what one wanted to do, but the whys and wherefores of doing it. An instinct for literature and a natural ear for words are invaluable aids. Nevertheless, there were, I found, innumerable details, and important ones at that, in which I needed instruction. It is by no means impossible to give oneself, unassisted, a liberal education; it is, indeed, far more difficult to give oneself a special and practical education. But much wasted time and disappointment are spared an eager writer who finds a sympathetic and tolerant teacher.

Throughout these early years I spent months in

discovering for myself the simplest rules which an experienced craftsman might have shown me in a few days or weeks. Yet, even if I had been strong enough to attend the Southern schools of the period, I should have been scarcely more proficient in the special training I needed. When years afterwards, in Edith Wharton's autobiography, I read of "the friendly critic," "with an exceptionally sensitive literary instinct," who had "tried to model the lump [of her first work] into a book," and who had taught her "whatever I know about the writing of clear concise English," I felt one of my rare reflective pangs of envy. For no such good fortune attended my start in letters. My only critic was within. My only teachers were my natural distrust of the easiest way and my natural sense of proportion and harmony. Slowly, and with infinite patience, in spite of my frail health in childhood and early youth, which placed any thought of a systematic education beyond my reach, I set myself to overcome problems of technique, and to feel my way, step by step, while I was learning to write better. The method is tedious; it is extravagant; it is unnecessary in an age when, all around us, learning is forced down unfit throats reluctant to swallow it. Still, if the way is indirect, it leads somewhere, I thought, as I picked up *The Romantic Comedians,* and traced the road I had followed. That road had led somewhere in the end, and it had ensured long remembrance. For all that one has acquired by hard endeavour is apt to stay by one.

But here, it would seem, difficulties begin to arise. There is always the danger, in speaking of a literary method, that one may appear to exaggerate its importance. Technique is valueless, I believe, so long as one regards it as technique alone. Only after one has acquired it, and forgotten the acquisition, does a formula lend itself to adaptation and become an incalculable help to a novelist. Nevertheless, it is well for every aspiring writer to serve either a voluntary or involuntary apprenticeship. Of late it has become the fashion to disparage artistry; but that may be because there is, nowadays, so little among us. In our whole-hearted retreat to the Neanderthal, we have taken both the short cut and the easiest way. It would be astonishing, if we had not grown used to the almost daily exhibition, to watch the agility with which modern novelists spring up to discredit the art they have attempted to practise. One might imagine, indeed, that the proudest boast of many contemporary writers is that they are able to excel in pursuits that have nothing to do with the profession of letters, or even with reading and writing. To have won acclaim as a pugilist or a stevedore or a ditch-digger or a bull-fighter or a public enemy would seem to be the best introduction to modern literary success. However humiliating the fact may appear to those of us who still cherish a discredited art, that fact, as a matter of psychology alone, at least raises an interesting point. Does this increasing abasement of the mental before the physical processes of life rest upon an obscure masochistic impulse in the modern literary mind? Does the symptom spring from a subjective pathological source? Is it an effect of the prolonged maladjustments of what we call civilization?

Perhaps. Perhaps not. In the days of my youth such degradation of intelligence before instinct would have been classified as simple derangement of the reasoning faculty. I had always wished to be a novelist. I cannot remember that I had ever wished to be anything else. And, at sixty, I find the barbaric fallacy of the present as alien to my mood as I ever found, at twenty, the sentimental fallacy of the eighteen-nineties. Intellectually, I had made my break with tradition when, in 1897, I published *The Descendant*. I had made my break for good and all; I was free, but I was also unanchored. I was ignorant alike of my own direction and the points of the compass. Revolt had not yet been subdued to the civilized uses of irony. I felt only that I must write of a rebel against society; and, in the Virginia of that time, there were no rebels against society, or, at least, there was not one in the circles in which I lived and moved and observed. One plan alone remained, and that plan would take me away from the scenes I knew best, away from Virginia, out into a different world, where I should be a permanent exile. This plan was imprudent; it was even hazardous; but, at twenty, I was attracted by imprudence and hazard. And it was the only possibility ahead of me. I could not write sentimentally about anything; and yet I could not, at that age, write otherwise about Virginia. The background was too close; the setting was too much a part of my interior world. Creation had always been easier for me than the act of transcribing; but literary creation demands a foreground, a middle distance, and a perspective. When one is too near, or too much involved in the subject, values are displaced, and the fluid contours are apt to solidify freezingly. So it seemed easier, on the whole, for me to place my social outcast in unfamiliar surroundings than to violate the probabilities by thrusting a revolutionary mood into the conservative pattern of Virginian culture.

If I linger over my first novel, it is because the germ of my future work, as well as my philosophy of life, lay hidden in that immature effort. I made my central figure an outcast escaping from rural Virginia, and with the opening sentence, "The child sat by the roadside," I felt him stir and breathe and become animate. Crude as the book is, and I am under no delusion that it is important, there was never in my mind the slightest doubt as to the reality of Michael Akershem. From the moment I first saw him sitting, ragged and barefooted, in the dust and sunshine, he spoke and acted with the dynamic motive of revolution. The book, which I began when I was eighteen, though it was put aside for three years before it was finished, was abrupt, unreserved, and inadequately written; but it was, I think, well constructed and completely realized as an actuality. From the first paragraph to the end, the figure of Michael Akershem was inevitable. "Why did you make him blink his eyes?" a reader once asked me; and I could only answer in astonishment, "I did not make him blink his eyes. He was blinking them when I first saw him, as a child, by the roadside."

In the more than three years that passed between the day I began and the day I finished this book, I had lived through a deep and tragic experience, in the loss of my mother. During her last illness, when I felt that the end was approaching, I had suffered an agonized recoil from life and death, and, for the years while this state of mind endured, I put aside not only the book I was writing, but, as I thought then, all future interest in fiction. Not until two years after her death could I bring myself to take out the six early chapters and read them over again. Because I had grown older, and no doubt more critical, I saw then that the work was that of an amateur, an adolescent blend of precocious thinking and childish emotionalism. But the little outcast in the story still seemed to me to be vital and true, and while I felt my interest reviving, I found that the child had impressed himself upon my imagination. My personal grief appeared more to have intensified than diminished his hold on my mind; and by a singular transmutation of feeling, he seemed to have shared in my sorrow, and to have grown in stature, through my experience of life.

When I trace his story today, I find that it leads me back to my early interest in science and economics. At that time, I was an eager student of John Stuart Mill, and I had successfully passed an examination in political economy, given me privately (for girls were not, of course, admitted to the classes), by that distinguished scholar, my old friend, Dr. George Frederick Holmes, of the University of Virginia. After Mill, I discovered other and more or less radical social philosophers. I read, among many others, Adam Smith, Malthus, and

Sir Henry Maine, and with enthusiasm for his brilliant style, Walter Bagehot. Finally, by accident, I stumbled upon *Progress and Poverty* in a second-hand book shop, and I was deeply stirred by the analysis of poverty in the opening chapters.

But the book that influenced my mind most profoundly in youth was *The Origin of Species;* and it was in response to this benign and powerful inspiration that I conceived my first novels. Before I had finished them, I had read so widely in the writings of science that it required total immersion in the centuries of sound English prose to restore my natural ear for rhythm and my instinct for style. Huxley, as everyone is aware, was a master of his own style and manner; but, for the most part, especially when I recall the numerous translations from the German language through which I patiently ploughed my way, I am convinced that a close and prolonged reading of science is an almost fatal exercise for an author who is trying to write better. It is needless to say that legal English as an influence is even worse; for what beginning author, in his right mind, would ever read legal English? Years afterwards, when I discovered the British philosophers, I regretted that I had not approached science indirectly through metaphysics. For several of the English and Scottish philosophers, and, in particular, one Irish bishop

philosopher, were masters of style. But apart
from the writing, I feel an obligation to the discipline of scientific method, which enabled me to
build a philosophy of experience upon the firm
theory of evolution.

Happily, this is not meant to be an analysis
of *The Descendant.* That earnest endeavour has
been long forgotten, and it is now numbered among
the disinherited. I have mentioned the book only
because Nicholas Burr in *The Voice of the People* was the natural companion of my earlier tragic
rebel. And it was, I suppose, the little dust-storm
stirred up by my first book that brewed the general scheme of my Virginian history of manners.
Whether people liked what one wrote, or failed
to like it, was no great matter. But that one should
write the truth of life with a single mind and a single conscience, appeared to me, at the moment, to
matter profoundly. So I determined that I would
write, not merely about Southern themes, but a
well-rounded social record of Virginia from the
decade before the Confederacy down to the period
in which I was then living, which happened to be
the beginning of the twentieth century. My subject
seemed to me to be fresh, and most certainly it remained untouched; for Southern novelists hereto-
fore had been content to celebrate a dying culture.
Yet the historic drama of a changing order and

the struggle of an emerging middle class were set against the many personal dramas of individual frustration. The world was full of fermenting processes, of mutability and of development, of decay and of disintegration. The old agrarian civilization was passing; the new industrial system was but beginning to spring up from chaos.

And so it was inevitable that one of the earliest books in this series should concern itself with political changes. In the final defeat of the aristocratic tradition, power had fallen from the hands of the Virginia planters into the hands of what used to be called "the lower orders," and an insurgent democracy was harnessing this power of its own peculiar designs. From this group, then, and this democracy, my central figure, the son of a "peanut farmer," and a "poor white," would thrust upward, as I saw the underprivileged of that epoch thrusting upward to political authority all over the Commonwealth. An eager and open mind in the South, which moved reluctantly away from the old culture, from the old formal manner of living, could not easily escape into fantasy. The tempo of transition was in the air, was in the industrial uprising, was in the whole psychology of an epoch. Heartily as one might regret the old ways, or hate the new, one choice alone was offered the artist and the thinker. To advance or retreat, these were the only alternatives. One must either encounter reality or accept the doctrine of evasive idealism.

My earliest novels had been steeped in the mood of revolt; and the vehemence of this mood had carried me away from the South to the more shifting elements in a large city. Now, in returning to Virginia, I discovered a social revolution in the moment of triumph. Although this revolution was less articulate than the wider rebellion of ideas, it was perhaps more successful, since it worked through the orderly forces of government. And here, moreover, I told myself, was the raw substance of realism. Here were tragedy and comedy and the perpetual conflict of motives. I would treat of the continual dissolution and renewal of social patterns, not in the South alone, but wherever man has built his temporary habitation in a universe that is indifferent or hostile. In the midst of a crumbling order, how could I depict established conditions? How could I render a permanent way in the flux and reflux of material disintegration?

While I was writing *The Voice of the People,* I spent many months in old Williamsburg, which was my Kingsborough. I knew the place; and I came to know every buttercup in spring on the courthouse green. I knew well also the originals of Judge Bassett, of General Battle, of Miss Chris, and of Marthy Burr. Amos Burr, I had known not once, but many times; and I owe to his Kingsborough prototype my knowledge of the peanut in every stage. His incurable pessimism was the natural philosophy of all farmers, in the South and elsewhere, who depend on the elements. In Nicholas, his son, I have embodied the social upheaval and the rise to power of the poorer rural class in Virginia. "Miss Glasgow's democratic fight in realism," wrote Stuart P. Sherman in his essay *The Fighting Edge of Romance,* "is incarnate in the little red-haired hero of *The Voice of the People.* Realism crossed the Potomac twenty-five years ago going North."

So far as I am aware, this novel was the first work of genuine realism to appear in Southern fiction. Others there may have been, but I was not aware of them. The political situation was reproduced with scrupulous fidelity, and I describe, without exaggeration, a Democratic State convention in our Commonwealth. In the late eighteen-nineties, I had driven over a mountain to a convention in Roanoke, where I was smuggled into the opera house by one of the door-keepers, and sat hidden behind the stage throughout the proceedings, a single feminine observer in an assemblage of more than a thousand men. As a girl, I found all this amusing and exciting; now, after more than thirty-seven years, both the effort and the incident appear incredible. What a mountain of endeavour was required to make one realistic novel.

But, in this chronicle of manners, I soon found that my historical conscience was involved even more deeply than my developing literary instinct. Never again would I adhere so firmly to the superficial truth of external surroundings. Richmond, as a background for the second half of the book, is a most faithful copy of the Richmond I had known in my early youth. The social customs, the manners, the easy familiarity of a long-established order which had fallen upon evil times—all these aspects of a changing moral climate were rendered exactly. Every house that I mentioned was then standing, every tree, every stone, every brick. Even the pictures in Nicholas Burr's library were actually hanging on the walls of the "Governor's mansion" in the Capitol Square.

Yes, it is all true, and, as truth does not invariably seem, it is all plausible. Everything in the book is real to me, except the fact that I wrote it. For *The Voice of the People* belongs, with *The Battle-Ground* and *The Deliverance,* to another life.

THE ROMANCE OF A
PLAIN MAN

WHEN I was very young, old Church
Hill in Richmond held for me a mys-
terious fascination. Not only did it
seem as far away as a place in *Grimms' Fairy
Tales,* but it was clustered as thickly about with
legends as an enchanted forest. That quarter, I was
told, had once been the most fashionable part of
our city. Shaded parks, looking strangely haunted,
overhung glorious views of James River, where
boats sailed to unknown ports, which appeared in-
credibly distant to my childish vision. In the centre of the straggling streets, St. John's Church still
presided over the parish; and my child's history
book, compiled by a Southern lady who had given
all to the Confederacy, informed me that in old
St. John's, Patrick Henry had made his immortal
demand for liberty or death. I had been told also,
and I considered this utterance far more romantic,
that, when his admirers wished to elect Patrick
Henry Dictator of Virginia, as a suitable reward
for his rhetoric, Archibald Cary, of the poetic

name, had threatened to leave his dagger in the dictator's heart.

Because I was taken there so seldom perhaps, the trip to Church Hill was always an adventure. In order to reach the top of the ascent, we drove very fast down one long hill, and then very slowly up a second long hill. But, in my memory at least, the arrival was never disappointing. More fascinating even than St. John's Churchyard was the great house with the walled garden, which spread in green terraces far down the steep hillside. In my childhood this house was still occupied by a Miss Van Lew, who was supposed, mistakenly no doubt, to have been a Northern spy during the War. True or false, the rumour appeared to have had little effect either upon the lady or upon the community in which she lived in peace, though shunned, I had heard, by her neighbours. This sinister reputation made her, it is needless to say, only the more romantic as a heroine of fable. I had a confused idea, indeed, that the disapprobation she aroused resulted, not so much from her legendary spying activities, as from her later habit of entering an annual protest, when she paid her taxes, against the tyranny of taxation without representation. Once, when I was playing in the street outside her garden, I caught a fleeting glimpse of her through the gate, and she seemed to be a frail, shrunken, white-haired old lady, who looked as if she would never have the heart to hurt a mouse. When I inquired about her at home, I was told that she was not only suspected of spying for the Yankees, but that she was known, on better authority, to be the first woman suffragist in the South. And I recall also that when I asked what a woman suffragist was, I learned that it meant having a vote, but not ever, ever, no matter how tired you might be, having a man offer you either his arm or a chair. From this germ of enlightenment, sprang, I think, though I cannot be sure of the fact, the image of Miss Lydia Bland in my story.

The Romance of a Plain Man, first published in 1909, parallels a yet earlier novel, *The Voice of the People.* Both books continue my chronicle of manners, which is integrated by the major theme of social transition. Whereas, in the earlier story, I had dealt with the poorer class from the rural districts, in the present novel I followed the upward way of the working man in the city. The two books were meant to run a parallel course, from the middle of the eighteen-seventies well into the first decade of the twentieth century. To render a whole society in defeat, it was necessary to deal, not only with outward and inward processes, but, even more specifically, with both rural and urban communities. In this sequence of novels, I have tried to delineate opposite manners of living. I have tried also, as far at least as it was possible in an accurate picture, to avoid sentimentality, as well as the superficial picturesqueness of "local colour." My single motive was to analyze the enduring fibre of human nature under the law of continuity and the sudden impetus of dramatic occurrences. Family ties had linked me so closely to the past that I had always felt myself to be attached to its permanent structure. In my blood there were remote inheritances from the past three hundred years in Virginia; and when I recorded events that occurred before I was born, I seemed to be writing of things that I had actually known. For all that, I was resolved in mind, and disposed by inclination, to concentrate more upon universal impulses than upon provincial behaviour.

Because I have painted an actual scene, my novels are fundamentally American in conception. Whatever their failings may be, they cannot, with truth, be called either derivative or imitative. Even my method was one that I worked out for my own needs. If we except the first invigorating inspiration of the great realists, which passed quickly, my work has owed little or nothing to any literary influence. I was content to write of life as I had lived or observed or imagined life to be.

Beyond this, I wrote solely in obedience to some inward pressure. And it is as true today as it was when I accepted my early call to a vocation that I have written chiefly because, though I have often dreaded the necessity, I have found it more painful, in the end, not to write.

It cannot be denied that I have omitted to deal with the later immigrants, and with what would seem to Virginians to be the rootless life of the prairies. But fate, by an accident of birth, decided that issue. I could write only of the scene I knew, and this scene had been furnished, however inadequately, for the past three hundred years. The figures in the landscape belonged to the stock that we call Anglo-Saxon. Our past was an English or Scottish past; in the beginning, the life I knew at first hand had been roughly hewn out of a wilderness by English or Scottish pioneers. Even if there were validity in the doctrine, prevalent among contemporary novelists, that the culture invented by the newest immigrants represents the only genuine American culture, there would still be no reason, in my opinion, for attempting to portray a confusion of strains with which I had few ties either of association or inheritance.

For this reason, among many others, I have refused to be swept into the current stream of patriotic ethnology. And, for reasons other than this, I have

refused to be carried away by the present grotesque
revival in Southern fiction, which is a remote logical result of our earlier hallucination, the sentimental fallacy. The sense of horror is not only
human, it is a useful, and entirely legitimate, literary *motif*. None of us, I imagine, is completely
immune from its power. And Heaven forbid that
I should set out as a champion of that forlorn
hope, human behaviour. One may admit that the
Southern States have more than an equal share of
degeneracy and deterioration; but the multitude
of half-wits, and whole idiots, and nymphoma-
niacs, and paranoiacs, and rakehells in general,
that populate the modern literary South could
flourish nowhere but in the weird pages of melodrama. There is no harm in the fashion, one surmises, until it poses as realism. It may be magnifi-
cent, indeed, but it is not realism, and it is not
peculiarly Southern.

But this perennial curiosity about corruption
may be, in fact, merely a survival of the eight-
eenth-century appetite for "thieves' literature" or
"scaffold confessions." We may recall what Defoe
himself, the great father of that school, as well as
of the modern novel, had to say in his preface to
Moll Flanders:

"The moral, 'tis hoped, will keep the reader
serious, even where the story will incline him to

be otherwise. . . . There cannot be the same life, the same brightness and beauty, in relating the penitent part as in the criminal part, because there is not the same taste and relish in the reading, and indeed it is too true that the difference lies not in the real worth of the subject so much as in the gust and palate of the reader." And so, in the words of an honest writer, and the founder of literary realism, we may leave the whole question of horror and the fascination it exercises in fiction.

Although men novelists, from Defoe onward, have never hesitated to write of women in the first person singular, and certainly Moll Flanders and Roxana are among the most vital women in the English novel, I felt, even while I was engaged on the work, that, for a woman novelist, it was a mistake to let Ben Starr tell his own story. Yet I could not do otherwise. So the novel had come to me; and whenever I had tried to change the form of a book, I had found that vitality would soon begin to languish and fail. This question of the proper use of the first person has been frequently discussed in criticism, and either approved or condemned according to the preferences of the critic. For my part, I have always thought that the method contained almost insurmountable disadvantages, even when it was employed by the great masters of prose fiction. In the beginning, how-

ever, my intention was to write a romance of the
ordinary, and to treat, with a faintly satirical
flavour, a series of adventures in the democratic
society of our time. The time, it is needless to say,
easily lent itself to such handling.

Our story opens in the year 1875; and at that period the upward swing of recovery had scarcely begun, and Richmond was still bearing, one imagines,
all the external signs of a devastated region. On all
sides there must have been adventure among the
ruins. In *The Voice of the People,* I had already
portrayed the effects of social recovery in the provinces; but I had written of Nicholas Burr from
the point of view of a spectator. I had made him
a part of the general transition, and his emergence
into politics had been handled objectively. In *The
Romance of a Plain Man,* since I was dealing with
very nearly the same social changes, common to
all parts of Virginia, I wished to make the approach from within outward, and to combine the
participant and the narrator. That the method had
its defects, I was aware, when it first presented
itself. Yet I knew that it had, also, its merits, and
it seemed to me, perhaps mistakenly, that this particular technique, which is associated with heroic
enterprises, would lend a sharper edge, and occasionally an ironic tone, to this realistic romance
of an average man of good will. I was not, there-

fore, entirely unprepared for the result. A natural simplicity in the child's mind keeps little Ben solid and living; but, as he grows up, he becomes more shadowy, until at last he exists less as a personality than as a continuous stream of memories and reflections. Nevertheless, as he gradually recedes and diminishes, the impressions of the scene, and the whole surrounding set of circumstances, are endowed with a more substantial actuality.

In reading the story again, after almost thirty years, I am convinced, not so much by its inner truth, as by its authentic rendering of unwritten history. The picture of the place and the time, which had altered little through those two special generations, are as exact as if I had unrolled one of the old prints of Richmond. Whatever may be said of Ben Starr as a character in fiction, the community in which he lives, and the people who move about him, appear to me to acquire the vividness lost by the narrator as he unfolds his recollections. If I seem to press in this point, it is because this is the only one of my novels (since the second half of *The Voice of the People* does not reach back so far into city life) in which I attempted to reconstruct each precise detail of the old Richmond which was still standing in the last quarter of the nineteenth century. When I grew up in the eighteen-nineties, that past still existed, and it was not until a wave of prosperity engulfed the State at the turn of the century that progress, more fatal than poverty, destroyed the lingering charm of the older culture.

All the opening scenes on Church Hill are faithfully rendered. I knew the little house, with the door giving on the street, where Ben Starr lived as a child. I knew the Adams's house, as I have said before, and I had played among the gaily coloured leaves in St. John's Churchyard and on Chimborazo Hill, overlooking James River. It was on Chimborazo Hill that Ben first met General Bolingbroke, whose remote original I had known also. From a respectful distance, I had known, too, Dr. Theophilus Pry, and the outside "office," where he taught his classes, at one end of a small three-cornered garden in lower Franklin Street. But the earlier scenes on Church Hill were those I remembered most vividly. They came back to me through a long vista, from an almost obliterated yet unforgettable past. I remembered Ben Starr's mother, though not his father, and I met, in my younger years, both Mrs. Cudlip and Mrs. Boxley, who frequently came in to sew for us by the day. Accompanied by my coloured Mammy, who enjoyed funerals, I had even attended, at a distressingly early age, the burial of Mrs. Cudlip's mother, though I was restrained from following the plumed hearse, drawn by a pair of black horses, to the poorer cemetery on the wrong side of town. Sally Mickleborough, except for her name, which was that of one of my great-grandmothers, was a creature of the imagination; and her mother's romantic story was pure, though not improbable, fiction. Yet, if I invented Sally, she was, in a measure at least, a mingling of all those characteristics we used to think of as especially Virginian.

All my life, but particularly as a child, I was attracted by the submerged neighbourhood known as "the old Market." On the rare occasions when I was driven past it, on my way to Church Hill, I would imagine myself lost and wandering under the grim arches of the market and through the mean streets that surrounded it, where, oddly enough, living appeared to take on increased excitement and colour and liveliness. It may have been this childish association that impelled me to let Ben Starr relate his own narrative; but I think my one and only literary adventure with the first person singular is more likely to have been the sad result of my youthful fondness for the heroes of romance. Yet were there no heroic qualities today? I speculated, not without irony. And where, for the matter of that, were all the lions in the path of victorious industrialism? At the present time, I

confess, the theme appears far less attractive to me
than it appeared in the first decade of the twentieth century, when I was hemmed in, between the
pale realism of New England and the florid romance of the South and West. Looking back, indeed, over the years, I find that the merit of the
story, if it has merit, depends upon the truthful
record in these parallel volumes of the stubborn
retreat of an agrarian culture before the conquests
of an industrial revolution, and the slow and steady
rise of the lower middle class, which was also the
working class in the South. Because I wish to place
the stress on this particular motive, I have found
it impossible to avoid repeating myself throughout
these reviews of my work and of the fundamental
purpose with which it was first conceived.

Taken together, then, the careers of Nicholas
Burr and Ben Starr appear to cover, with the
imaginative privileges of fiction, the history of a
decline and rise in Southern civilization. Although it was a time of change, it was also, perhaps because of this shifting surface, a time of opportunity. Once again, power was defying Jeffersonian theory and adopting Jeffersonian policy.
The average man was at last in the saddle, and
since average men compose so large a majority,
democracy was already marching with banners. In
that place and period, the rise of Ben Starr was

far from unusual, and if the rise and fall of Nicholas Burr seemed unusual even then, he himself was a logical product of that universal law which tends, in all ages and societies, to make some few men superior to circumstances. All over the South, as the industrial system displaced the agrarian aristocracy, men were springing up out of obscurity and forging ahead into prominence. The history of Ben Starr was scarcely more than a wheel within the larger wheel which held the centre of balance. The significant drama is the drama of external occurrences, and the mind of the narrator is used chiefly to limit the scope of the background, and to shed a revealing light on the general pattern of life. As the part of the story-teller became thinner and vaguer, I felt that the picture of the changing world about him gathered reality, and that one heard through his consciousness the rapidly awakening tumult and confusion of the new South.

VIRGINIA

VIRGINIA," which reproduces the period from 1884 to 1910 in a history of manners, was intended to be the candid portrait of a lady; and nowadays, as I am made increasingly aware, the lady has become almost as extinct as the dodo. Still, her gracious semblance, delicately moulded in wax, may be found in the less frequented wings of museums, where archaic fashions are reconstructed and preserved in glass cases. The lady's dresses, her mantles, her petticoats, her bonnets, her veils, her slim, fragile shoes —all these are exposed to the curious or incurious gaze of the sightseer. But the grace, the beauty, the vital essence, the shimmering radiance which made her the ornament of the ages, survive now, if anywhere, only in the boundless realms of fable and allegory. It seems amazing to me, when I reflect that so short a time ago as the second decade of the twentieth century, when I was working from life on this portrait, the Southern lady had not entirely disappeared from her once familiar surroundings. In their latter years, I had known

77

many of these survivors of a more decorative era; and because I admired them, somewhat pensively, as one admires the rare art of a finer period, I have tried to interpret the vanished lady with sympathy, though not entirely without that cutting edge of truth which we call irony. Although the gentlewoman has existed, more or less precariously, in all parts of the world, the native climate and soil of the South have combined with its particular institutions to furnish for her species an appropriate background of fauna and flora.

The theme of *Virginia,* or at least the germ of the idea, was contained in a phrase. Many years ago, on a mild autumn afternoon, I was walking with a friend along a street called Bolingbroke, in one of the older aristocratic towns of our Commonwealth, when we passed a woman of later middle age, who looked at us with eyes of a faded flowerlike blue and the smile of a wistful Madonna. As she went by, my friend glanced after her and sighed softly, "How lovely she must once have been!"

That was all, but it was enough. I never heard her actual name; yet when she returned, by and by, to haunt my imagination for years, she brought with her her own unalterable name and story. I knew her life as well as if I had lived it in her place, hour by hour, day by day, week by week;

and gradually, I found that her image was blending in contour with the figures of several women I had known well in the past. From the first paragraph in my novel, there was never the faintest haze or obscurity in that long perspective. Not ever was I obliged to pause or wonder what should come next in my narrative, or whither it was leading me. I knew infallibly how she would act or speak, respond or recoil, in any situation. From the moment when I passed her living figure in the street, and then lost it, she came and went in my mind through an atmosphere of inevitability.

Although, in the beginning, I had intended to deal ironically with both the Southern lady and Victorian tradition, I discovered, as I went on, that my irony grew fainter, while it yielded at last to sympathetic compassion. By the time I approached the end, the simple goodness of Virginia's nature had turned a comedy of manners into a tragedy of human fate. I saw her first as she came to Miss Priscilla Batte, on that May afternoon, in the year 1884, clothed in an innocence which saddened the old teacher, who gazed, prophetically, into the future. "Would life," she asked herself, "yield nothing more to that radiant girl than it had yielded to her or to the other women whom she had known?" And then, vaguely frightened, "But if ever a girl looked as if she were cut out for happiness!"

On that warm and fragrant afternoon Virginia was wearing a dress of white lawn, with the close-fitting sleeves and narrow waist of the period, and the ruffled flounces were looped up with bows of blue ottoman ribbon. Her dark hair was wound in a wreath of braids round her head, and broke into a mist of little curls over her forehead. Her eyes, set in black lashes, were the colour of wild hyacinths. From that instant until the end, when she stops on the porch of her house and looks back at the street, before she enters, as one might look back before the door of a prison, she was as close to me, and as real, as my heart or my nerves.

And this accent of inevitability emphasized, for me, the whole scene of the town I have called Dinwiddie. It was as if the vividness of Virginia's interior truth had brought to life every person and object, every house and street, that composed her surroundings. Through her perceptions and impressions, I came to know them intimately, one and all; I felt that they were endowed with a significance which separated them from all other persons and houses and streets. They had been there, alive and waiting, throughout the years; and no sooner had Virginia's story taken shape in my mind than all the details of the background appeared before me in complete actuality. I saw the rectory, with the two great paulownia trees guarding the door, and the market where the old slave block was still standing, while Mr. Dewlap sold his white pullets to Mrs. Pendleton. The town was real; it was humming with the subdued energy of the past. All the people that lived in it were solid; they were whole and round; they moved about and cast shadows. As soon as my foot touched the earth of Dinwiddie, I was at home in the place. I knew what I wanted; I began to set the mood and furnish the landscape with figures. All I had to do was to summon the people from the old houses, and leave them free to spin the situation out of themselves and their own destinies. For this was a true story, which created its own play of events. A superimposed plot would have distorted the structure of circumstances. An artificial brightness would have shed confusion into the light of day. And just as in my thoughts this drama slowly evolved, so the tragedy, which was virtually contained in the theme, must unfold from itself, and develop in obedience to its own conflicting motives.

Whenever I attempt to recall the actual writing of *Virginia,* and to recapture the mood in which the book was conceived, I find myself moving again in an imaginary world which was then more real to me than the world I inhabited. I could not separate Virginia from her background, because she was an integral part of it, and it shared her validity. What she was, that background and atmosphere had helped to make her, and she, in turn, had intensified the life of the picture. Every person in Dinwiddie, from the greater to the least, was linked, in some obscure fashion, with her tragedy, and with the larger tyranny of tradition. In this provincial climate the characters were all so closely associated that I had no perception of assembling a group or distributing the figures. They were there before I came, just as the town was there, just as Virginia was there, just as the place and the people had come together for a dissolving moment in time. All these people possessed, not only their special personalities, but their surroundings as well; and I could do little more than select and eliminate, and arrange the subtle details of composition and the movement of circumstances. For Virginia was more than a woman; she was the embodiment of a forsaken ideal. Already, when I wrote of her, she was beginning to pass into legend; and even man, who had created her out of his own desire, had grown a trifle weary of the dream-images he had made. But, in passing, she still wore the spiritual radiance that invests the innocent victim of sacrifice. Her only armour was goodness; and her fate was that almost inevitable martyrdom which awaits pure selflessness in a world where self-interest has always been the governing power.

Nevertheless, this martyrdom is not without its own particular irony. For Virginia Pendleton, prepared for the actuality by Miss Priscilla Batte's Academy for Young Ladies, which taught reading, penmanship ("up to the right, down to the left, my dear"), arithmetic, geography, history, deportment, and the fine arts, was the perfect wife as man had invented her, and as he still believed that he cherished her. The pathos of it was that neither in life nor in my novel was she a weak character, as some undiscerning readers have called her. On the contrary, she was a woman whose vital energy had been deflected, by precept and example, into a single emotional centre. She was, indeed, as I had known her in one I loved and pitied, the logical result of an inordinate sense of duty, the crowning achievement of the code of beautiful behaviour and of the Episcopal Church.

A few weeks after my novel was published, I received a visit from one of the perpetual widows of the South, who might have served as a model for Mrs. Pendleton. Her reproachful face was as melancholy as a lost cause, while her crape veil flowed to the hem of her skirt, which was still modest in length.

"Do you really think, my child," she inquired, with patient sweetness, for she had known my mother, "that a young girl could be inspired to do her duty by reading *Virginia?* I do not deny that there is truth in your book; but I feel that it is a mistake for Southern writers to stop writing about the War." Then, sighing pensively, she continued: "If only I had your gifts, I should devote them to proving to the world that the Confederacy was right. Of course, I know that even the best novelists are no longer so improving as they used to be; but I have always hoped that either you or Annie Cabell's son would write another *Surry of Eagle's Nest.*"

This was in the year 1913, and the next time I saw my perpetual widow she was cutting out pyjamas in the crowded rooms of the Red Cross. Enthusiasm had bloomed afresh in her pensive face, and had she survived the immediate martial need of pyjamas, she would probably have devoted her ample gifts to proving that still another war was "right." She died, as she would have wished, in the midst of a righteous conflict, and even her type has disappeared as utterly as the sense of duty or the code of refined conduct.

To return to the neglected town of Dinwiddie

in Virginia. Caught between the training camps of war and the spurious prosperity of munition factories, the town would scarcely be recognized by one who had known it before the post-war disintegration had set in. Like other Southern cities, large and small, Dinwiddie has sold its charm to industrialism, and has grown modern and commonplace. Industrialism, as usual, has proved to be a poor creditor. Yet, underneath the mechanical invasion, one may still discover, here and there, a fragment, or it may be only a reminder, of the forgotten art of manners. Turning aside from the main-travelled street to the sunken pavements, shaded by old trees which have escaped the political axe, one surprises an elusive spirit or poetry of place, which speaks, not of the present, but of the deeper life that was lived here in the past. For me, since I return so seldom, the town evokes the three animated years when I was writing *Virginia*. My Dinwiddie was saturated with the breath of old streets and old houses, with the moist smell of bricks sinking into the earth underfoot, and the dry, drifting dust of wood that had rotted away. The place in my mind had wholeness, solidity, the capacity for extension. I knew the look of the streets; I knew the people who walked through the sunlight and shadows, and came and went in and out of the doorways; I knew the whispering, provincial undercurrent of rumour. The community had its network of veins, but the vital fluid in its veins flowed from the subjective life of Virginia. Although she moved freely in her world, and her world moved freely within its natural confines, Virginia remained always at the centre of gravity.

Because the town was thus inextricably linked with Virginia, I felt that it must control its own separate and individual sphere of activity. One could really know and understand the girl and woman only after one had known and understood the external setting of her story. It was necessary, therefore, that the Treadwells should appear not less real than the Pendletons, that Miss Willy Whitlow, the sewing-woman, should be made as convincing as Virginia or as Oliver.

For this reason, I remained dissatisfied until I had settled each character in a fitting place. It was not sufficient to know the town. I must know also where and when my various persons had lived in this town. It took me days, for example, to find the proper dwelling for the Treadwells. After all these years, I can still savour the taste and smell of old Dinwiddie, while I roamed the streets in my urgent house hunting. For a whole afternoon I had searched, when, just at sunset, we turned the corner into Bolingbroke Street, and I stumbled upon the exact house that I wanted. The instant my eyes fell on the narrow brown front, I expected the door to open and Cyrus Treadwell to come out on the shallow "stoop" and descend the steps to the pavement, where, much to his annoyance, children were playing hop-scotch. Tired but happy, I sank on the bottom step of the adjoining house and surveyed the end of my search. "The Treadwells live here," I said, with conviction. "If we wait, we shall see Cyrus or James come out of the door." And, strangely enough, while we sat there in the flushed air of the sunset, the door opened, as I had known that it would, if only we had patience, and a long, lank man, who might have been Cyrus himself, came out on the stained marble porch and passed, with his splay-footed walk, down the steps and up Bolingbroke Street. Presently a light glimmered through the small window-panes, and I knew that Mrs. Treadwell, who had once been vain and pretty, but was now drab and slatternly, was buttoning her basque of alpaca and fussing with the untidy ashen fringe on her forehead.

Sitting there on the step next door, I could see, in imagination, the Treadwell family gathered in that darkening house behind the closed door. I have always ranked the Treadwell group among my more successful characters; and from the moment they entered my mind, each one of them was animated, for me, by a special identity. It is true that Susan, the variation from stock, seemed to me too nearly normal to be interesting to the psychologist; but I thought of the others as the sort of human beings Balzac might have liked to depict; and the figure of Cyrus awakened in me something of the thrill with which a novelist exclaims, "I have caught him alive!" At least one critic has said that my treatment of Cyrus and the coloured washerwoman struck the first "daring" note of Southern realism; but, it may be because the incident was true, I did not regard either Cyrus or the episode as in any sense daring. In the same way, when I pictured the old man on his back porch spitting down into the bed of miniature sunflowers, I was trying to subordinate sentiment to veracity in Southern fiction. So I had observed the original Cyrus, and so I caught him, as it were, in the flesh and the act. It is one of the eternal contradictions of civilization that the Southern culture which could produce the noble figures of the rector and Mrs. Pendleton could produce also, upon occasion, the ignoble Cyrus and his cowed and slovenly wife.

But Dinwiddie, with all that it contained, supplied at once a physical boundary and a part of the general march of events. The density or subtlety of texture, the variations of light and shadow, the mutable effects of time, and the depth or shallowness of the human figures that passed, in relief, against continuing tradition—all these semblances of the actuality were meant to isolate and interpret one of the perpetual conflicts of life. If Virginia is absorbed into the Victorian tradition, even more compellingly she has absorbed that tradition into her own consciousness. But the larger conflict is not with tradition; it goes further, and sinks deeper, until it becomes the eternal warfare of the dream with the reality. In this warfare, all the persons in the narrative have taken arms, even Cyrus, even poor Miss Willy Whitlow ("How could she go out sewing by the day if she lost her religious convictions?" asked Mrs. Treadwell), but especially Oliver, who is burdened by imagination and the temperament of an artist. In another period, Oliver might have been a second Marmaduke Littlepage; but, in Dinwiddie of the eighteen-eighties, he remains disappointed though not disillusioned. Oliver, the idealist, had wanted his dreams, and nothing, not even idealism, can afford to live upon dreams alone.

Always, while I was writing this novel, I had a sense of feeling my way from the personal tragedy of Virginia toward the larger impersonal tragedy of the years. It is not only that Virginia was once young and then is young no longer; it is not even that she was once a girl, a happy wife and mother, and at last an outgrown mother and a deserted wife. Among women, ancient or modern, such a lot is far from uncommon. But, in my narrative, there is always time, the arch-antagonist, pursuing, engulfing, and finally breaking down her resistance to Fate. In reading the book now, I seem to feel the very curve and fall of the years bearing her down. And beneath the slow or rapid flight of the seasons, I hear also the muffled undertones of a refrain which runs continually throughout my work, "the pathos of life is worse than the tragedy." It may be that Virginia's earlier portrait is the more "speaking" to me because I drew her appearance from a description of my mother when she was very young. For my mother also had looked, I was told, "as if she were cut out for happiness." And like my mother, Virginia, who was the perfect flower of Southern culture, was educated according to the simple theory that the less a girl knew about life, the better prepared she would be to contend with it. "The chief object of her upbringing, which differed in no essential particular from that of every other well-bred and well-born Southern woman of her day, was to paralyze her reasoning faculties so completely that all danger of mental unsettling, or even movement, was eliminated from her future." Love comes, as fleeting as ecstasy, and her strength, for she is not weak in fibre, hardens into the inherited emotional patterns. As wife and mother, she approaches perfection; but it is a law of our nature, as of all nature, that change only endures, and the perfect mould must be broken. Still, she remains as she was in her youth. The years may tread her down; but they are powerless to destroy that inviolable essence which is the self within the self.

Her children, to whom she has sacrificed her whole existence, grow beyond her; her husband deserts her; and yet, confirmed in goodness, she stands immovable where she has stood for a quarter of a century. From the beginning, she has never demanded; she has never followed her own desires; she has been incapable of altering the design of her life. Although the irony has grown fainter, it is still there at the end, interwoven with the pathos and the tragedy. She has lived for others so long that she has lost even the blind instinct of self-preservation. "And there was nothing to do today; there would be nothing to do tomorrow; there would be nothing to do next year, or the year after that. She saw, now, with a piercing flash of insight, so penetrating, so impersonal, that it seemed the result more of some outside vision than of her own uncritical judgment, that life had treated her as it treats those who give but never demand. She had made the way too easy for others; she had never exacted of them; she had never held them to the austerity of their ideals." Yet the tie between her and her only son was unbreakable; and in emphasizing the strength of this bond, whether as an ideal or an actuality, I am rendering the truth of an individual experience.

But time, her antagonist, had conquered. Minute by minute, with the slow wash of the tides on a beach, time had worn away her loveliness, her innocence, her flushed expectancy, her radiant belief in life, which was dimmed but never extinguished. One after another, like sands drifting, all the little graces, all the small things that made up the sweetness of life, slipped by and were gone. More slowly still, under those soundless waves of the years, the larger things also began to pass from her, the dependence of her children, the imperative desires of her husband, the multitude of daily services that had once filled the present emptiness of her heart. Nothing but constancy was left to her, and constancy, when it has outlived its usefulness, is as barren as fortitude. Time had not crushed her, but, little by little, the years had nibbled away the very roots of her life.

Nevertheless, goodness still clung to her, goodness and patience, and that lost instinct of a lady.

Stronger than constancy, more invulnerable than fortitude, this deep instinct remained what it had always been, the controlling influence of her nature. A mere anachronism, as it now appeared to the vulgar or the undisciplined, it yet provided a sustaining motive when she confronted the triumphant mistress of her husband. At that meeting, for the first time in her marriage, she comprehended that she was fighting, not a woman alone, but the whole structure of life. "And with this comprehension, the almost imperceptible hostility which had flashed in their glances when they met had seemed to die down, and the triumph which had been on the side of the other woman appeared to pass to Virginia. Then, because it was impossible to say the things she had come to say, because even in the supreme crisis of her life she could not lay down the manner of a lady, she smiled the grave smile with which her mother had walked through a ruined country, and taking up her muff, which she had laid on the table, passed out into the hall."

Perhaps, as I have said elsewhere, my having known and pitied the original Virginia may have added a more intense pathos to the chapters treating of her return to Dinwiddie and her aimless wandering over the scenes of her youth. But it is true that these chapters moved me as only the realities are able to move the heart. For Virginia was more to me than a character in a book, though even as a character in a book, I find her wholly animated and consistent from the first page to the last. In writing of her, and indeed in writing of all the inhabitants of Dinwiddie, I felt that I was swept on by a current in which I was immersed at the very moment when I tried to interpret its meaning. Throughout this novel, I was possessed, or so I thought at the time, by that pre-established harmony between material and medium which is the one unqualified reward in the pursuit of a difficult craft. To move freely through an imaginary universe, in command of circumstances, yet subject to the laws of continuity—this is success, whether that success be recognized or unrecognized, for the biographer of life.

In this book, the influence of the realistic school of fiction is still evident. I have followed that technique in fullness of substance and in accumulation of detail. Yet the ironic overtones, the relentless logic of events, and the application of modern theories in psychology, all these, I think, were in advance of the period in which I was writing. "Such books may be true to life," complained one Southern reviewer, "but we should hesitate before placing them in the hands of our trusting wives." Well, after all, I was not, in the year 1913, writ-

ing either for Southern reviewers or for their
trusting wives.

Although the stage of this drama is Virginia's
consciousness, yet, as I went on, it seemed to me
that the external setting, with its varied figures
and its closely woven fabric of circumstances, had
become a part of her inner landscape. Her mind
reflected the changing shapes and colours of her
surroundings, as a commemorative tapestry of the
past repeated the minute effects of the seasons, including the small animal lives and the slow sequence of flowers. Certain scenes or incidents
blazed out, for me, in high relief, while others
sank back into the neutral tones of ordinary experience. Virginia, in her girlhood, waiting for
love and marriage. Virginia riding back from the
fox-hunt, after her three days' jealousy, with a
bedraggled brush, which had once been grey, tied
to her bridle. "She had neglected her children,
she had risked her life; and all for the sake of
wresting a bit of dead fur from Abby's grasp."
And again Virginia, after Harry has been near
to death with diphtheria, and she had saved him,
shut in alone with her child through the days and
nights, while Oliver had been at Atlantic City
with Abby. " 'Poor Oliver,' Virginia said gently.
'He must be anxious.' Yet, even while she uttered
the words, she was aware of a sudden sense of

unreality, as if she were speaking of a person whom she had known in another life. It was only three days since she had parted from Oliver, but in those three days she had lived and died many times."

Such, then, is the smaller personal drama within the larger drama, which remains impersonal and aloof. For as the years are treading down the life of Virginia, so they tread down, not less ruthlessly, the feminine ideal of the ages. More slowly, but quite as inevitably, they were closing over the great tradition, which was older even than Victorian manners, since it had sprung from the dreams of Adam, and had been preserved in the eternal forms of religion and legend. And so, in this minor tragedy of a woman's life, we see the effects of the years wearing away and obliterating a single dream of identity, an individual illusion of happiness, which is encircled by the wider curve and sweep of time, as time wears away and obliterates yet one other discarded mould of perfection. For fantastic as her image appears nowadays, the pattern of the lady had embodied for centuries the thwarted human longing for the beautiful and the good.

LIFE AND GABRIELLA

L IFE AND GABRIELLA," the concluding volume
in this chronicle of manners, is a companion study to a previous novel, *Virginia,*
which had portrayed woman as an ideal conforming to Victorian tradition. The present work is
concerned with woman as a reality; and it is concerned, too, with the complete and final departure
from that great tradition. Although Gabriella
lived only a decade later than Virginia, a whole
era of change and action, one of the memorable
epochs in history, separated the two women. The
younger woman, a character of native energy and
independence, blessed with a dynamic philosophy
and a quick relish for the immediate, was, in a
measure at least, the symbol of an advancing economic order.

Dissimilar as they appear, both novels represent
characteristic stages in Southern culture. In the
middle 'eighties, when Virginia grew to womanhood, the past order still lingered on as a state of
mind; and the Southern woman, who had borne
the heaviest burden of the old slavery and the new

97

freedom, was valued, in sentiment, chiefly as an ornament to civilization, and as a restraining influence over the nature of man. But the next decade was scarcely over when one of those momentous revolutions of opinion, more drastic in the end than any revolution of facts or of institutions, had already begun. Insurgent youth, hardened by the poverty and deprivation of the post-war years, had damaged, though it had not as yet entirely broken through, the fixed pattern of custom. Even in the feminine sphere was self-assertion, somewhat gradually but beneficently, displacing self-sacrifice. Sentimentality, both as a rule of conduct and as a habit of mind, was yielding to the more practical, and the more profitable, virtues of common sense. For the preceding generation, custom and change had been alike circumscribed by the boundaries of a defiantly reconstructed Virginia. But the early 'nineties saw the first noticeable flight of the migration northward. It is true that, after the end of the Confederacy, a thin scattering of Virginians had found it wiser, if less patriotic, to fatten in the land of strangers than to hunger on the lean acres of family estates. Yet not until the sharp-set appetite of youth had demanded a livelihood did an exodus start among the sons, though seldom among the daughters, of the lost heritage.

Because alike of historical accuracy and of logic, it seemed to me appropriate to end my history of transition with an escape such as this from defeat. Nevertheless, in writing of life in New York, I have been careful to deal only with Virginians, and with their transplanted loyalty to their native culture. Wherever they may settle, it is typical of Virginians that they should remain parochial in sentiment. So rhetorical indeed, upon occasions, has become this perambulatory ancestor worship that it has produced a hybrid, and singularly unattractive, type of professional Southerner. It follows, therefore, that the circle Gabriella enters in New York is quite as provincial, and even more clannish at heart, than the family circle in Richmond. Only when disaster has overtaken the mushroom prosperity of these exiles, and when Gabriella is thrown bodily upon her own slender resources, does she discover her hidden strength and reach her true level of circumstances. And, meanwhile, from her earliest revolt, in the deep Victorian gloom of the front parlour in Hill Street, to the moment, some eighteen years later, when she follows O'Hara to the Pennsylvania Station in New York, the whole train of events is observed entirely through the eyes and the consciousness of Gabriella.

After a stretch of years, when I turn back to this

novel, I find myself living again in New York, where I spent a part of every year immediately before the First World War; and I see again the lights blooming out of the trees in Central Park, and the flushed outlines of the towers on the horizon. This is the only one of my books that was not written in the upstairs "study," where I sit now, at my great-granduncle's desk, in the old grey house on a forgotten corner in Richmond. Although the opening chapters dealt scrupulously with everyday life in the South, all these scenes were set down beside a window that looked out on the clustering foliage or bared branches around a thin blue lake in Central Park. Because I lacked that wordless evidence of my background, an inherited knowledge, I was particular to verify the look of every street, of every house, and of every external detail. The Fowlers' house, with the brownstone front, in the Fifties, was one I had lived in during my first visit to New York; and I had spent some two months on the West Side, in a dreary apartment-house, then called the Windermere, where Gabriella finds temporary refuge after George has deserted her. Madame Dinard, the modiste, was an actual person, and the fashionable house of Dinard was an actual establishment. When Gabriella moved down to one of the dwelling-houses in London Terrace, in West Twenty-third Street, I went over, from top to bottom, the house she selected, on the pretence that I might consider renting it for a year; and while I was working on the latter half of my story, I gave over many hours to a vigilant wandering up and down the old streets in that quarter.

And just as the scene was constructed from minute observation, for I was engaged then with the history of a period, so the human figures in the neighbourhood were drawn from a shifting multitude of visual impressions. Of them all, the improbable figure of Ben O'Hara is the only one that conformed to an original model. But for an accidental acquaintance with his counterpart, it is unlikely that Gabriella's break with the past would ever have assumed the shape it wore at the end. Because in this book I was painting directly from life, it could not have been otherwise in her truthful biography. Like a faintly satirical echo, I can hear my old friend, James Lane Allen, dissenting across the years: "Would any Southern lady have so far forgotten herself as to run after a wild Irishman?" Well, perhaps. Or perhaps not. But I have noticed that Southern ladies, even in the novels of James Lane Allen, have had a way of doing unaccountable things. In my own opinion, Gabriella was, as she was meant to be, far from extraordinary. Without any great endowment of beauty or charm or intellect, she possessed character and courage, sincerity of purpose, and an approach to life that was fundamentally intelligent. It was my idea to dispense, as far as possible, with any exceptional advantages. Yet I lacked, since this is a frank confession, the daring to make her simply plain and good. Bad women are almost as easy in contemporary fiction as they are in fact; but since *Jane Eyre,* no novelist has had the courage to make a heroine good and plain and beloved.

Well, my chronicle was ended. For better or for worse, it was over and done with. Probable or improbable, the task I had so long ago set myself was accomplished, and I was now free to dismiss my history of Virginian manners into an unheeding world. The period I attempted to cover extended from 1850 to 1914, and the work on the series had occupied me from 1899 until 1916. Although I had done the best that I could at the time, I was far from sure, when I had finished my sequence, that I could not have written it over, and have written it better, from beginning to end. I had grown in the writing, and—or so at least it appeared—America had grown with me. While I was gathering experience, and I was in my early twenties when I began to assemble material, all around me the once firm bonds of the genteel convention were beginning to loosen and to give way.

By the outbreak of the war, indeed, intimations

of truth, though not the whole truth, had become no longer forbidden in fiction. Yet we were still far behind the great post-war liberation in morals, when every novelist, and almost every biographer, began eagerly to tell all the things that can be said only in print. Fortunately or unfortunately, this record of a vanished culture contrasted with a slowly maturing culture was written under the old literary bondage, when there were words, and when there was, moreover, a whole indecent idiom, that simply could not be spoken aloud. If this necessary restraint has perhaps "dated," as they say nowadays, my chronicle of manners, yet this restraint had kept my chronicle more faithful to the language of the time and of the place it recorded. Be that as it may, with this final volume, I had exhausted, I knew, my earlier vein of social history in the form of fiction. Whatever I might write in later years would be in another field, and in response to an entirely new creative impulse.

When I turn and glance back over the way I have come as a novelist, I see the whole, not as a continuous curve, but as a straight line, bending here and there, which leads from one vanishing-point to another. From the dawn of my intelligence, I had known what I wished to do. I had, as the phrase runs, followed my star. Although I have not been happy (what creature with imagination could be happy in a suffering world?), I have been always interested and often amused. This summary is concerned, however, not with my life as a complete personality, but with the separate path which led, wavering now and then, but always recovering its level, in the direction of a single artistic endeavour.

In following that way in retrospect, conforming to its sudden curves, as well as to its steady level, I am forced to return, now and again, to the sources of my identity as a writer. I had not in the beginning, and I have not now, the slightest interest in fiction as a trade. Only as a form of art has fiction ever concerned me.

My first severe disillusionment followed, I think, the shock of discovering that, in America, and perhaps everywhere, literature was regarded not as an art, not even as a profession, but as a business. Although fiction, in the 'nineties, had not yet developed into "big business" of the present time, the commercial instinct was rapidly dominating the whole profession of letters. A disturbing surprise came when I was taken to one of the annual receptions of the Authors' Club, a well-entrenched body in the latter years of the nineteenth century. This was before I had published my first book, and at the moment, indeed, the manuscript was receiving the slow consideration of the house of Harper, in Franklin Square. Now, at last, I thought eagerly, I shall learn something of authorship. But instead of the ripe wisdom I had expected to gather from the bearded meteors of our literary firmament, I listened, with incredulous amazement, to an animated discussion of the prices paid by the leading magazines. My disappointment was ridiculous, but it was also acute. Nevertheless, when I have since compared this conversation with the talk of the intelligentsia in our post-war world, I have perceived that, though it sounded tedious to my youthful ears, the general attitude was not without dignity. The leaders of that none too brilliant period may have appeared dull; they were indubitably pompous; but, for all that, they were, and they stayed completely aware of this, men of letters. They were not bothered by the necessity of pretending to be anything else, whether sophisticated barbarian or rustic buffoon; and not one of them would have stooped to apologize for, or to explain away, his honourable calling. If they innocently encouraged one another in mediocrity, as Charles Lamb remarked of an earlier literary circle, they remained invulnerable to the assault of the untutored and the blatant. Occasionally, it is true, a gifted or influential "one-book author" would contrive to break through the iron defense of "the old guard," but it was not until a whole generation of novelists had been lost and found, that the republic of letters surrendered unconditionally to the cult of the amateur.

The Descendant, an obvious product of immaturity, had been rejected, after an unconscionable time, by two leading publishers, who disapproved of what they called "unpleasant subjects." Depressed but undefeated, I had then turned, in humility, to an inferior house, which could not, I assumed, feel an obligation to "lead" anywhere; but I had soon found that the superior and the inferior presented a united front to any sort of "unpleasantness" in any novel. To these publishers, my manuscript had gone, humbly and honestly, bearing my own name; but a friend in need, who submitted the book to Harpers, was prompted by some innate discretion, or perhaps by a subtle understanding of publishers, to offer the manuscript anonymously, and in person. Fortunately for me, one of the critics for that eminent firm proved to be so lacking in discernment that he pronounced *The Descendant* an unsigned book by Harold Frederic, the author of a then popular novel, with a depressing theological flavour, entitled *The Damnation of Theron Ware.* With this unmerited endorsement, my book was immediately accepted; and when it was at last published, still anonymously, my publishers assured me that the reception was favourable, although that particular brand of favour aroused, I think, my incurable distaste for notoriety in every form. The reviews in general were agreeable, even in Great Britain. It is true that the South disapproved, but I had lived long enough in that section to know that the South would instinctively disapprove of the living.

Although I have said elsewhere that *The Descendant* has dropped permanently out of print, this does not mean that the book is safely dead even nowadays. In spite of its incredible innocence, and in spite of its scientific vocabulary, of which, at twenty-two, I felt myself to be vastly proud, some human vibration has kept the story, or its legend, at least partly alive. I am told, on good authority, that the volume is still read in college libraries; and, at intervals, I am called upon to verify the distinguishing marks of the first edition. Does Du Maurier's *English Society* head the advertising pages at the back of the book? Or is this position occupied by another Du Maurier volume, *The Martian?* And, stranger still perhaps, I could not answer these questions, until, some years ago, I had glanced over my assembled "firsts" in the library of a collector. Just as I had never valued my manuscripts, after the books were securely printed and bound, so I have never troubled to keep in touch with my straying first editions.

As a very youthful author, heartened by moderate success, I made several resolutions, to which I have been more or less faithful throughout the years. Happily, I had cut my literary eye-tooth on the sweets of notoriety, and I had learned, once for all, that to me the taste of it could never become palatable. Like all other writers, earnest and young, I had craved fame; but fame, as I saw it then through a rainbow mist, was a far-off, and, in all likelihood, a barren blessing. I had, even at that age, few illusions concerning posterity. I have, in the present, no illusions whatever regarding posterity's discrimination in literature. So far as I can foresee, there is small reason to assume that the literary taste of the future will be superior to the literary taste of the present. For the past forty years, I have watched, with edification, and not without sardonic amusement, a seemingly endless procession of stillborn masterpieces welcomed, acclaimed as surpassing fruits of genius, and allowed to slip overnight into oblivion. In all these years, the larger stage of American literary opinion has been set with a perpetual comedy of errors, a continual apotheosis of the average. Yet, incredible as it must appear to the wandering faculty of reason,

I still nourish an instinctive feeling that books "live" because of their intrinsic merits, not because of some fortuitous conspiracy of events. And, although I am without hope or illusion of what we call immortality, so illogical on this subject is the mind of the natural writer, that I would rather be read by a dry-as-dust minority in an as yet unborn future than by an alive and active contemporary generation.

And so, knowing my own attitude, however unreasonable that attitude might seem to be, I resolved that I would never compromise with success. Not that I was consciously writing either for "antiquity," as Charles Lamb exclaimed, or for an even more ambiguous posterity. When I reduced my purpose to a formula, I understood clearly that I was considering merely my own disposition, and also, it may be, my own limitations. I wanted, above all other benefits, freedom to live in, room to grow in, and leisure to dream in. The modern world, as I found it, was hostile to all these desires. I would, therefore, take of the past and the present alike only as much as I needed; and this meant that I must keep myself free alike from thwarted motives and conflicting endeavours. I liked money, but I liked other things more.

Two things, and two things only, were requisite to my identity both as a human being and as a writer

—an intense immediate experience, and the opportunity to translate that experience into forms of creative imagination. I could, therefore, wait while I was working. If the future held anything for me, I could wait for it. If the future held nothing for me, I could wait for it quite as well. I have had disappointments; I have had heartburnings; I have had resentments; but these were all as ephemeral as they were futile. And, however disagreeable such sensations may have been while they lasted, they were never strong enough to overcome the force of my original determination. In concrete shape, these past resolves (never to write for magazines; never to enter a contest; never to write for money) have helped me, even when I was unaware of their influence, to conserve my vitality as a writer. It is no exaggeration to say that I feel younger at sixty than I felt at twenty, when I was oppressed by my own and the world's sorrow. For my spirit has not yet seemed to decline. Ideas are still thronging; and "something tells me," as beguilingly as this same ageless "something" told me in youth, that my mind and my pen are now engaged on a masterpiece.

When other novelists occasionally lament to me that they have "written out of ideas," or that their creative energy has diminished after their first few books, I can only wonder why my experience has been so dissimilar. For life to me has been a continual becoming. Apparently, time has not lessened either my interest or my enthusiasm. Nor have these qualities been damaged by anxiety, or heartache, or the unhurried practice of letters. Maturity has been, for me, more active than immaturity; and, in many ways, even more inclined to protest and experiment. I had hoped that each passing year would tone down the edges of oversensitive nerves; but, instead, I have found that a capacity for vicarious suffering is, if anything, greater than it was in youth. Although a kind of cheerful pessimism, lightly turning into ironic amusement, has hardened to fortitude, both my sympathy and my resentment are still as easily aroused as they ever were in the past. I have never lost the old irrational sense that, by some sinister fate, I had become in part responsible for the evils of a world which, like the Shropshire Lad, I had never made.

Whether this ancient sense of sin is the late revenge of that Calvinist conscience I inherited, on the paternal side, but refused to accept, or whether it is the result of an acute physical susceptibility, I have never stopped to inquire. Another remote Calvinistic survival, perhaps, which I shared in youth with none of my acquaintances, has become less erratic, it seems, in modern experience. This is an instinctive, and no doubt illogical, feeling that I had no right to seek happiness for myself in a scheme of things where so many mortal creatures, both man and beast, were enduring even upon earth the extreme tortures of hell. Pain anywhere, without purpose and without hope, a single wilfully tormented animal, has denied, for me, the perfect harmony of the spheres. Not only have I entered into such pain, with which I had nothing to do, and which I would have given my life to alleviate, but I have become, in mind at least, a part of that suffering, as if a connecting nerve held me bound fast to the source of another's anguish. Yet I have known, too, a feeling for beauty that was almost an ecstasy. I have had moments of rapture; I have had moments of exaltation; I have had moments of mystic vision. The only moment, indeed, that I have not seemed to share, or to touch as it passed, is that proverbial moment of awe, when the heart dreads the end and fears death.

If this too individual analysis appears to have no direct bearing upon my work as a whole, and little upon each novel considered alone, it has a place in my theory that all creative writing is an extension of personality. To understand any work of imagination, good, bad, or indifferent, one must first understand something of the underlying real-

ity from which it has been distilled. And I may
confess that I have written so frankly in these
prefaces only because I have borne always in mind
the thought that this Virginia Edition is limited
both in scope and in numbers. It has seemed to me
only natural to assume that the subscribers who
have made these books possible in their immediate
form would be not uninterested in the origin of
my ideas, and sympathetic with my views, alike of
the art of fiction and the scheme of the universe.

With these unseen companions, among critics
and readers, who have stayed near me in understanding throughout the years, I feel an intellectual kinship which is stronger than gratitude. The
casual or the faint-hearted will drop away with
the changing fashions, but I may take, I think, an
honest pride in the thought that the circle of my
friendly readers has not diminished with time. For
novelists at least, the world is easier nowadays than
it was at the beginning of the century, when some
of us first came together. Much good ballast may
have been thrown overboard, but we have discarded also not a little that was a mere hindrance
to veracity. Since, even in the year 1897, I was,
in the present sense of that abused word, a modern, it is natural that I should have welcomed with
interest the whole modern movement in letters.
For the modern process, as I take it, means a

breaking up on the surface of facts, and a fearless exploration into the secret labyrinths of the mind and heart. That way, as I follow its windings in perspective, is concerned less with the vehicle of experience than with the perpetually escaping spirit of the thing we call life. In the past, we have been too often satisfied to imitate and embroider our standard patterns of consciousness, while we have neglected both the essence of the mind and the true nature of circumstances. But it is the interior world that contains the deeper verities and the sounder realities.

And even in the novel, we are beginning to demand a larger presentment of life than may be condensed into a formalized depiction of love. We are beginning, indeed, to demand a faithful rendering of existence, and a more pointed analysis of our emotions, as well as a closer and more sceptical examination of accepted facts. It is true that the novel, in common with other and less adaptable forms of art, appears to have attained, and it may be to have passed, its highest fulfilment. In an earlier day, it was finer, perhaps, than any exact transcript of life we may achieve in the future. But the restless mood of the modern temperament cannot fit its energies into the smooth and rigid moulds of an age that was less complex and more stable. Although we may have again nothing so

good as the simple forms we have known in the
past, still we have reached the end, I think, of that
fruitful road, and we must at last turn either toward a more promising vista or into a blind alley,
which is empty of all but the winds of doctrine
and theory. There remain, as I see the problem,
only two choices. Will the art of fiction grope its
way into vacancy until it declines eventually upon
the dead centre of power? Or will it recoil upon
itself, and, exploring still deeper, escape into a new
province? With all its faults and failings, the contemporary novel remains alive, however inadequately; and, from my point of view, even inadequacy is redeemed by the eagerness with which
this vital medium strives for a more intense consciousness, and for a closer agreement with the
realities of experience.

It would appear, then, that the balance of advantage lies with the present. Yet we cannot deny
that, in spite of all we have gained in substance
and in certainty of handling, we have left behind
us, in the dark ages of faith and sentiment, that
special faculty of pure narrative which makes fiction interesting. Many, though by no means all,
contemporary novels seem, in a reflective vision,
to resemble not a chain of mountains, but a monotonous level. They are without variation, and
yet when one seeks to grasp an integral idea, the

pattern dissolves into words. Still, in the hands of a great artist, this newer subtlety, or even vacancy, may become luminous with suggestion. When I discovered Proust for myself, I remember thinking, with delight, "Here is a way out of the woods." Virginia Woolf is never flat or inanimate; and though Joyce is often unreadable, one cannot but admit that, if *Ulysses* is frequently dull, it is, none the less, a dull work of genius. But all these writers have a quality, though it may be only a touch, of pure genius. They are, in any case, so vastly superior to the multitude of their imitators that they should be held exempt from entangling alliances. In America, we do better when we are satisfied to remain ourselves, and American. I believe, indeed, that the recent revival of the historical novel, reaffirming our past, and the heroic tradition of our origin as a people, may be regarded, by and large, as a revolt of natural human interest against the monotony, the staleness, the sordidness, and, above all, against the incredible dullness of the average stream of consciousness in fiction.

The great novels, it is needless to remind ourselves, have never, in any place or period, belonged to a limited trend, or been circumscribed in scope by a fashion. For the great novels have marched with the years. They are the contemporaries of time. Yet, to one who has been an observer, as well as a practitioner, of fiction for at least a part of two generations, the most spectacular reversal of the situation would seem to have occurred, not so much in our requirements of literature, as in our general attitude toward the arts. As Mr. George Arliss has remarked of the theatre: "Perfection in art has gone. So many successes in the theatre today are really accidents. A young playwright makes a 'hit,' and then disappears. Why? Because he has struck upon a particular subject that is so dramatic to him that a 'hit' automatically happens. Then there is nothing left for him, for he hasn't prepared for his profession."

So it is with the theatre, and so it appears to be with the sister art of prose fiction. How many contemporary works, applauded as masterpieces for a season, have dwindled to mere literary accidents when they are reviewed against the long procession of letters! Even as a beginner, I had seen the folly of this temporary acclaim, and my hope had been, not to write one successful book and retire, but to leave behind me, whether it was recognized or neglected, a solid body of work.

So far, I have dealt almost entirely with the benefits of the past; and when I turn about and contemplate the superior advantages of living in our own time, I shall appear, no doubt, to contradict my previous assertions. But, in fact, it is not so.

Although I may like better many aspects of other periods, both in art and in the actuality, still, taken together, and allowing for the defects of its qualities, I should prefer unquestionably to live in the age we have with us. In spite of its mental encumbrances, which are great, and of its moral disillusionments, which are infinite, all other demerits are overbalanced by the present total eclipse of our former optimistic moonshine. For I was never an optimist, although I was "a modern" at a time when the later, and more fortunate, moderns had not arrived, or were not even expected. In other and broader spheres than the province of letters, "not to look on the bright side" of things was regarded as irreligious in principle; and, in the nineteenth century, it was better to have achieved infant damnation than to be irreligious in principle. During the latter years of our era, and indeed until American idealism had been safely buried in Flanders fields, a belief in the happy end was as imperative in philosophy as it was essential in fiction. The universe, as well as a love story, must lead to romantic fulfilment. But only the older novelist, who has suffered under the artificial glow of the past American idealism, can appreciate the blessing of the liberty not to believe, and of the even more hardly won liberty not to be glad. By reason of a more honest relation to life, this freedom has brought about a less hypocritical approach to letters. Even the political intolerance of the present, a later manifestation of the religious hatreds of the Middle Ages, appears to be simply a democratic version of the immemorial ferocity against alien ideas.

If abstract or legal virtue has diminished—and we cannot, I think, deny that it has—we have gained, however slightly, in a closer kinship with all other forms of life, including the vast, and but partially understood, animal creation. This expanding fellowship is largely owing, it seems, to a decreasing smugness in our mental outlook, to a slowly declining anthropomorphic pomposity. On the one hand, we see a vehement exaltation of the barbaric, and on the other hand (paradoxes are common in history), we may observe, if we are endowed with a leisurely habit, the slow and reluctant widening of the humane consciousness of mankind. From the past, then, I should like, were it possible, to retrieve a few individual graces of culture, while I would, at any sacrifice, seek to preserve and develop the broader comprehensions of what we may call the modern point of view. I should like, most of all, to rescue from encroaching oblivion the forgotten virtue of good manners, which embrace so large a part of social morality. And by good manners, I mean a subtle delicacy of perception and behaviour which unites consideration for others with a regard for sensibilities different in fibre and quality from our own.

Certainly, I find it more agreeable to inhabit a world which, in spite of numerous impediments to happiness, permits its citizens, not excepting the best minds in universities, to speak a part at least of the truth as they know it. That has not always been so. In some places, notably in the South, it is not usually so even nowadays. Still, dismissal that is not followed by the rack or the stake is a change for the better. And I find it agreeable, too, since I was born, as my early books testify, without that special social instinct euphemistically labelled, class consciousness, to exist in a stage of the world's progress when class consciousness, in common with other inhibitions of personality, is looked upon with disfavour. There is evidence around us, to be sure, that this altered point of view has been accompanied by effects that are not wholly pleasant. But this is obliged to occur with any sudden changes in climate, whether they be moral or physical. When I was growing up in the South, such restrictions, embodied in rules that appeared to me to be absurd and unfair, not infrequently caused me annoyance, and, in particular instances, they worked for positive pain. At the present time, however, these limitations have more than passed away; they are almost forgotten. Pride of name or place has long since yielded to pride of pocket, and even pride of pocket is slowly giving way before the bleak democracy ensured by financial chaos.

In fiction, as in fact, this equalization may have needed general stability. Not to be equal, but to be paramount, is the ruling instinct of class, as of individual; and the proletarian in power becomes as despotic as the overthrown aristocrat. Yet it is the vehemence of living that provides the material of drama; and surely the immediate decade is a hopeful period for the dramatist, if only on the theory that the worse the world becomes, the more interesting it will be to observe and to write about. Although I would not consent to live my life over again, even under the most benevolent dispensation, I should like to begin afresh, and to carry through to accomplishment a new and entirely different body of work. The late Victorian sunset still lingered on at the turn of the century; and the road of the intellect was a well-beaten path, strewn with the impedimenta of settled convictions. An extravagant amount of energy had to be wasted merely in proving that things were not what they seemed, and that they were, in fact, seldom known by their right names. One could understand then what

Goethe meant when he exclaimed: "Thank God I am not young in so thoroughly finished a world!" But the young today are not troubled by convictions; they are not troubled by ideals, especially by the ideals of their elders. I envy them their early freedom from hesitations, but, in particular, I envy them their later freedom from pretences. The restraints of the present age are those less invulnerable barriers within; they are not artificial boundaries defining the beliefs or the prejudices of older authority.

Well, the end is not yet. And if the work ahead may be better, at least the work I have left behind me was integrated by an honest endeavour. Whether or not I gave the best that was in me, certainly I gave the best that I could in the special circumstances of the place and the period. Such as it is, there my work stands. I cannot alter it now. I am not sure that I would alter it now if I could. For I should choose not to turn back, but to go onward. I have gathered much from the past. All my mistakes were not made in vain; and I should like, had I the time and the opportunity, to profit by these mistakes in the future. For I have tried to take the longer view; I have put my faith in ideas; I have examined life, not from a remote angle of vision, but in the flesh, and with the pulse of the living. Always I have attempted, it may be unsuccessfully, to condense the results of experience and insight into a settled philosophy. To the imaginative artist, emotions, and even ideas, may be inconsistent in relation to art, but the truths of philosophy must, in a certain measure, be confirmed by the intellect.

Novels of the Country

An era changed, not rudely, but, as eras do change so often, uncomfortably. Power, defying Jeffersonian theory, and adopting Jeffersonian policy, stole again from the few to the many. . . .

THE MILLER OF OLD CHURCH

"THE MILLER OF OLD CHURCH," which was first published in 1911, parallels, in a measure, an earlier and more dramatic novel, *The Deliverance,* one of the scenes from country life in my history of the Commonwealth. In both books I have tried to depict the prolonged results of Reconstruction and the social transition, though *The Miller of Old Church* is placed in a later period and a different province of Virginia. In this locality, which is known as the Southside, the first settlers were almost entirely English; and twenty-seven years ago, when I studied the somewhat inaccessible scene of my story, the native speech was still tinctured with the racy flavour of old England. My rustic farmers, grafted from a robust Anglo-Saxon stock, were, in several instances, modelled after living figures of the time. In Abel Revercomb, I have portrayed the better type of the plain countryman who forged ahead, after the social upheaval, and became a power in the confident dawn of Southern democracy, before

the new fibre of that democracy had weakened
under the combined weight of ignorance and self-
interest. Mrs. Gay, who bore sorrow so nobly,
and Kesiah, who bore ugliness so submissively,
were both genuine products of the code of beautiful behaviour. Throughout the book there may
be found, if one cares to look for it, a certain
symbolic implication. Will the declining strain
of the aristocracy be enriched or depleted by
the mingling of social orders? Will the fresh
infusion of blood save the old way of living? Or
will it merely hasten the end of an incurable malady?

When I last visited the place, the original Jordan's Journey was still standing in its grove of
oaks, and the neighbouring white or black farmers
still brought their grist to be ground at the old
mill. Recently, however, I have heard that there
is only a chimney left of the house; and, after
more than a century of service, the mill also has
probably crumbled before the advance of what we
have agreed to call progress. If I were to return,
nowadays, to that once isolated community (which
is not the actual post-office of Old Church that one
may find on the map), I should discover, no doubt,
that the very features of the country had altered,
and that the effects of post-war psychology, if not
the science itself, had invaded even that primitive

region. But no. I may safely assume that I shall always see it unchanged. I shall keep my memories of the turning wheel under the crooked sycamore, of the chimneys of Jordan's Journey thrusting up from the reddened oaks; and, beyond acres of broomsedge, I may still look on the desolate loveliness of the horizon. If this novel has done nothing else, it has caught a dissolving slant of light on a scene that was rapidly passing away.

As the last of my books to be written in a fashion which I am obliged, however reluctantly, to call my earlier manner, *The Miller of Old Church* appears to me to be a rather curious blend of romance and realism. Although I had broken with tradition, I had not yet escaped entirely from the influence of its emotional patterns. I was still feeling the backward pull of inherited tendencies. In my next novel of manners, I was further on my way to complete freedom; but it was not until I began to write *Barren Ground* that I was able to orient myself anew and to respond to a fresh, and, apparently, a different, creative impulse. All that came after this period was the result of this heightened consciousness and this altered perspective. Unimportant as it may appear in a final summing up of actual endeavour, my later way of writing began suddenly, after a long apprenticeship to life, in a single intuitive visitation. But the struggle to this end had been difficult; and in order to understand the tradition and the way of life to which I had been born and from which I had broken away, it is necessary to glance back over the Southern scene and Southern literary conventions. . . .

Early in the dashing but decorous eighteen-eighties John Esten Cooke published his *Virginia: A History of the People,* an important and delightful little volume, which proved again that the sword was more prolific than the pen in the old South. Slipped in among more serious considerations—for war, not letters, is the proper business of the historian—we find a few brief discussions of Virginia authors; and toward the end of the book a modest chapter is devoted to *Virginia Literature in the Nineteenth Century.* After what he appears to regard more as a consoling than an encouraging view, Mr. Cooke, who was a distinguished novelist, prudently decides to explain away, not to praise, his subject.

"If no great original genius," he concludes, "has arisen to put the lion's paw on Virginia letters, many writers of admirable attainments and solid merit have produced works which have instructed and improved their generation; and to instruct and improve is better than to amuse. Whatever may be the true rank of the literature, it possesses a distinct character. It may be said of it with truth that it is notable for its respect for good morals and manners; that it is nowhere offensive to delicacy or piety; or endeavours to instill a belief in what ought not to be believed. It is a very great deal to say of the literature of any country in the nineteenth century."

That he lingers not to inquire but to moralize is sufficient proof, were one needed, of Mr. Cooke's sterling piety and settled convictions. For it was a period in which historians, like novelists, asked few questions and were able to believe, without prodigious effort, anything that was necessary. Speculation, when it flowed at all, ran smoothly in the safest and narrowest of channels. Novelists, especially when they were historians also, were required to instruct and invited to please; but they were not allowed to interrogate. Why old Virginia, with a mode of living as gay, as gallant, as picturesque, and as uncomfortable as the life of England in the eighteenth century, should have created, not a minor *Tom Jones,* the crown of English fiction, but merely *Cavaliers of Virginia* and *Knights of the Horseshoe*—this is a question which no Southern gentleman, however Georgian his morals or Victorian his manners, would have dignified with an answer. A minor Fielding may have been too much to expect. But it would seem to the cold modern mind that almost any readers who devoured them so voraciously might have produced a native variety of Mrs. Radcliffe, of Miss Jane Porter, or even of Mrs. Charlotte Smith. All these authors were with us in their solid bodies of masculine calf or modest feminine cloth. If our jovial grandfathers chuckled for a generation over *The Adventures of Peregrine Pickle,* our sentimental grandmothers shivered over *The Mysteries of Udolpho* and wept or trembled over the misfortunes of *Thaddeus of Warsaw.* Yet, while sentiment effervesced as easily as soda water, the stream of creative energy flowed, as thin and blue as skimmed milk, into the novel that was "notable for its respect for good morals and manners."

The one exception to such a statement is, of course, Poe. Mr. Cooke, after reminding us that Poe "passed his early life in Virginia," disposes of the matter with regret—or is it relief? "This great and sombre genius," he muses, "was rather a cosmopolite than a citizen of any particular State." This fact is certainly evident; but it seems to us nowadays that it should be only a way of measuring the wide and high quality of Poe's art. It does not deny the Southern essence in his genius, and Poe is, to a large extent, a distillation of the Southern. The formalism of his tone, the classical element in his poetry and in many of his stories, the drift toward rhetoric, the aloof and elusive intensity,—all these qualities are Southern. And in his more serious faults of overwriting, sentimental exaggeration, and lapses, now and then, into a pompous or florid style, he belongs to his epoch and even more to his South.

Having taken Poe, then, as the exception, we may return to our question. With the long inheritance of English tradition and culture behind it, why did the South (and this is especially true of Virginia) provide almost every mortal dwelling, except a retreat for the imagination of man?

It soon becomes clear that there are more answers than one to this question, and that each answer contains at least a germ of the truth. From the beginning of its history the South had suffered less from a scarcity of literature than from a superabundance of living. Soil, scenery, all the colour and animation of the external world, tempted a convivial race to an endless festival of the seasons. If there was little in nature to inspire terror, there was still less to awaken pity in hearts of oak. Life, for the ruling class at least, was genial, urbane, and amusing; but it was deficient in those violent contrasts that subdue the natural pomposity of man. Even slavery, a depressing spectacle at best, was a slight impediment to the faith that had been trained more to enjoy the fruits than to examine the character of peculiar institutions. Although in certain periods there was disseminated a piquant flavour of scepticism, it was a flavour that lingered pleasantly on the tongue instead of lubricating the mind.

Over the greater part of the old South (and this applies forcibly to Virginia, where the plantation group was firmly united) a top-heavy patriarchal system was adjusting itself with difficulty to unusual conditions. While this industrial process required men of active intelligence, it offered little hospitality to the brooding spirit of letters. It is true that in the latter years of the eighteenth century much able writing in politics began to appear. Jefferson, who touched with charm, and usually with wisdom, upon almost every subject that has engaged the mind of man, created not only the political thought, but the greater part of the Southern literature of his period. After his death, however, and particularly with the approach of the Civil War, political sagacity withered beneath a thick increment of prejudice. Philosophy, like heresy, was either suspected or prohibited. Even those Southerners (and there were many of these in Virginia) who regarded slavery as an anachronism rather than an iniquity, and looked ahead reluctantly to a doomed social order—even those pro-

phetic Southerners lacked the courage or the genius
that rides in the whirlwind and directs the storm.
Before approaching disaster, pleasure became not
merely a diversion but a way of escape. In the
midst of a changing world all immaterial aspects
were condensed for the Southern planter into an
incomparable heartiness and relish for life.

What distinguished the Southerner, and particularly the Virginian, from his severer neighbours
to the north was his ineradicable belief that pleasure is worth more than toil, that it is worth more
even than profit. Although the difference between
the Virginian and the far Southerner was greater
than the distance between Virginia and Massa-
chusetts, a congenial hedonism had established in
the gregarious South a confederacy of the spirit.
Yet in this agreeable social order, so benevolent to
the pleasure-seeker and so hostile alike to the in-
quirer and the artist, what encouragement, what
opportunity, awaited the serious writer? What
freedom was there for the literature either of protest or of escape? Here, as elsewhere, expression
belonged to the articulate, and the articulate was
supremely satisfied with his own fortunate lot, as
well as with the less enviable lot of others. Only
the slave, the "poor white," or the woman who had
forgotten her modesty, may have felt inclined to
protest; and these negligible minorities were as

dumb and sterile as the profession of letters. And
even if they had protested, who would have listened? Even if they had escaped, either in fiction
or in fact, where could they have gone? Pride,
complacency more human than Southern, self-sat-
isfaction, a blind contentment with things as they
are, and a deaf aversion from things as they might
be: all these universal swarms, which stifle both
the truth of literature and the truth of life, had
settled, like a cloud of honey-bees, over the creative
faculties of the age. That airy inquisitiveness which
frolicked so gracefully over the surface of thought
questioned the Everlasting Purpose as seldom as it
invaded the barren field of prose fiction. Religion,
which made so much trouble in New England,
had softened in a milder climate, among an Episcopal society at least, to a healthful moral exercise
and a comfortable sense of Divine favour. A noble
certainty that he was the image of his Maker im-
parted dignity to the Southern gentleman while it
confirmed his faith in the wisdom of his Creator.
Though the venom of intolerance had been ex-
tracted but imperfectly, the Protestant Episcopal
Church was charitable toward almost every weakness except the dangerous practice of thinking.
Moreover, the civilization of the old South was
one in which every member, white or black, respected the unwritten obligation to be amusing

when it was possible and agreeable in any circumstances. Generous manners imposed a severe, if mute, restraint upon morals; but generous manners exacted that the artist should be more gregarious than solitary.

II

Such, at least, is one answer among the many to our question: why should the old South have failed to produce great books when it produced great men in abundance? It is an answer sufficiently exact on the surface; but, even as we make it, we know that it requires another angle of vision. For as soon as we turn from imaginative literature to the uses of imagination in life, we discover that the creative art of the South was not a substitute for experience but experience itself, circumscribed and intensified. From a forgotten episode, an attitude, or a gesture, in the yellowed pages of an old diary, passion will start out, alive and quivering, charged, we are almost persuaded, with the significance, if not the subtlety, of metaphysics. Belief vibrates round us; the air thickens; and we are transported to an age in which the supernatural, or what we feel to be the supernatural, borrows validity from the worship that still enshrines it. Thus we come to understand that the whole scheme of living in the South was founded upon an idea of civilization, not the less abstract because it was expressed emotionally and rhetorically, but with little help from the written word. If literature was deficient in realities, life was full of what we may call, according to our habit of mind, exalted or evasive idealism. Life, indeed, was lived so completely in the open and in action, yet with so bright a flame of this particular aspect of idealism, that the need was seldom felt of a retreat into shadows. There was *katharsis,* as well as inspiration, in the cult of the hero as soldier and patriot, and in united surrender to a cause, however wise or impolitic, noble or reckless, that surrender may appear to the historian.

After the War, pursued by the dark furies of Reconstruction, the mind of the South was afflicted with a bitter nostalgia. From this homesickness for the past there flowered, as luxuriantly as fireweed in burned places, a mournful literature of commemoration. A prosperous and pleasure-loving race had been thrust back suddenly into the primitive struggle for life; and physical resistance had settled slowly into mental repression. Already those desperate political remedies which, according to the philosopher, begin in fear and end in folly, were welding the Southern States into a defense and a danger. From political expediency there emerged

alrous romances of William Gilmore Simms have
lost, if they ever wore, the colours of life, the Cre-
ole novels of George W. Cable are still suffused
with their own magic.

To those of us who are in accord with the artistic impulse we call Modernism, it is a relief to
find at last that the horizon of the American novel
is fluid, not fixed, and that there is a way of escape
from artificial limitations of material and method.
A fresh literary impulse in the South, which was
merely a single curve in the world movement toward freedom in art, had broken, not only with its
own formal tradition, but with the well-established American twin conventions of prudery and
platitude. Mr. James Branch Cabell spinning his
rhythms from iridescent illusion was still in harmony with the natural patterns of life. A long tradition and a thick deposit of hopes and fears had
flowered again in the serene disenchantment of his
philosophy. The austere perfection of his art, with
its allegorical remoteness and that strangely hollow ring which echoes the deeper human tones of
passion and pity, could have sprung only from a
past that has softened and receded into the eternal
outline of legend. Certainly it is an art that belongs by inheritance to the South, though it may
appear to contain no element we define narrowly

as Southern, except, perhaps, the gaiety and gallantry of its pessimism.

And yet it is true even with a novelist of philosophy rather than life that there must be a fourth dimension in every fiction that attempts to interpret reality. There must be a downward seeking into the stillness of vision, as well as an upward springing into the animation of the external world. For the novel, and indeed every form of art, no matter how firmly rooted it may be in a particular soil, must draw nourishment from the ancient instincts, the blood and tears, which are the common heritage of mankind. And because this is true of the South, as of the rest of the world, it is well to remind ourselves that art, to be independent, not derivative, to be adequate, compact, original, must absorb heat and light from the central flame of its own nature. The old South, genial, objective, and a little ridiculous—as the fashions of the past are always a little ridiculous to the present—has vanished from the world of fact to reappear in the permanent realm of fable. This much we have already conceded. What we are in danger of forgetting is that few possessions are more precious than a fable that can no longer be compared with a fact. The race that inherits a heroic legend must have accumulated an inexhaustible resource of joy, beauty, love, laughter, and tragic passion. To discard this rich inheritance in the pursuit of a standard utilitarian style is, for the Southern novelist, pure folly.

Never should it be overlooked that the artist in the South will attain his full stature only by preserving, at any cost, his individual integrity. Sincerely as he may admire the flat and vigorous novel of the Middle West, he can never subdue his hand to the monotonous soil of the prairies. That impressive literary movement has as little kinship with the Southern scene as it has with the special poetic forms that reflect so perfectly the frozen landscapes of New England. But in the restrained profusion of Mr. Cabell's art, or, to take another and a more recent writer, in the rich humanity, the mellow memories, and the singularly living prose of Mr. Stark Young, we find a genuine expression of the beauty which, however neglected and debased among us, is still natural to the thought and the literature of the South. If Mr. Cabell's delicate pursuit of the unholy grail wears, on high occasions, the semblance of allegory, Mr. Young's creative vision has the downward seeking and the upward springing of authentic reality.

It is easy to repeat that this artistic inheritance may be lost upon a race that has persistently confused emotions with ideas and mistaken tradition for truth. It is easy to repeat that a logical point of view is almost as essential to art as it is to philosophy. But these repetitions are not only offensive but futile. After all, what the South has known and remembered was a lavish, vital, and distinctive society, which, for want of a better phrase, we may consent to call an archaic civilization. Imperfect, it is true. For as long as the human race remains virtually, and perhaps essentially, barbarian, all the social orders invented by man will be merely the mirrors of his favourite imperfections. Nevertheless, there are arts, and the novel is one of them, that appear to thrive more vigorously upon human imperfections than upon machine-made excellence. Commercial activity and industrial development have their uses, no doubt, in any well-established society; but genius has been in even the most civilized periods a vagabond. And, with or without genius, the novel is more vital, and certainly more interesting, when it declines to become the servant either of sentimental tradition or of patriotic materialism.

III

Every observant mind nowadays must be aware of what we may call, without too much enthusiasm, an awakening interest in ideas; and a few observant minds may have perceived in the rising generation an almost pathetic confusion of purpose. In the temper of youth, we feel the quiver of expectancy, and an eagerness to forsake familiar paths and adventure into the wilderness. But where shall it begin? For what is it searching? Adaptable by nature, and eager, except in moments of passion, to conciliate rather than to offend, the modern South is in immediate peril less of revolution than of losing its individual soul in the national Babel. After sixty years of mournful seclusion, the South is at last beginning to look about and to coquet with alien ideas. With an almost disdainful air, the Southern mind is turning from commemoration to achievement. Noise, numbers, size, quantity, all are exerting their lively or sinister influence. Sentiment no longer suffices. To be Southern, even to be solid, is not enough; for the ambition of the new South is not to be self-sufficing, but to be more Western than the West and more American than the whole of America. Uniformity, once despised and rejected, has become the established ideal. Satisfied for so long to leave the miscellaneous product "Americanism" to the rest of the country, the South is at last reaching out for its neglected inheritance.

At this point it may be wise for the prudent essayist to pause and approach his subject with caution. The recently invented noun, Americanism, which appears so mild and harmless in print, reveals itself to the touch as a dangerous explosive. No other word in our language arouses so easily the fierce possessive instinct of criticism. So sensitive, indeed, are the emotions aroused by this label that when I attempted to treat it lightly in a thin vein of satire, I was taken to task by an indignant reader. Gravely, he charged me with harbouring what seems to be an "un-American" prejudice against a confusion of tongues. Yet nothing could be, in sober fact, more remote from my thought. On the contrary, I believe that America, if not the didactic term Americanism, is wide enough to include the diverse qualities in all the novels ever written by American novelists at home or abroad. Since the appearance of *Giants in the Earth,* I am disposed to add all the novels ever written by American novelists in any language; for Rölvaag had written a fine American novel in the Norwegian tongue. I am told that excellent American novels are written in Yiddish; and, for all I know, excellent American novels may be written in Greek, or even in Latin. Certainly, I see no reason why American novels, excellent or otherwise, should not be written in the South, where the English language is still in use. But they will be written, it is safe to prophesy, by those novelists who are concerned more with the quality of excellence than with the characteristic of Americanism.

For the Americanism so prevalent in the South today belongs to that major variety which, by reducing life to a level of comfortable mediocrity, has contributed more than a name to the novel of protest. After breaking away from a petrified past overgrown by a funereal tradition, an impressive group of Southern writers recoiled from the uniform concrete surface of an industrialized South. To mention a few names, among many, I should include Thomas Wolfe, William Faulkner, Allen Tate, Caroline Gordon, Marjorie Kinnan Rawlings, Hamilton Basso, Margaret Mitchell, Clifford Dowdey. But it is significant that, for the first time in its history, the South is producing, by some subtle process of aversion, a literature of revolt. Consciously or unconsciously, the aesthetic sense that surrendered to the romantic life of the past, and even to the more picturesque aspects of slavery, is rejecting the standards of utility in art and of fundamentalism in ideas.

Although it is true that there has been an advance in the South of what the world has agreed to call education, there is a corresponding decrease in that art of living, which excels in the amiable aspects of charm rather than in the severe features of dogmatism. If flexibility of mind has settled into earnest conviction, grace of manner has apparently hardened into a confirmed habit of argument. A new class has risen to the surface if not to the top. New prophets are creating new vices and denouncing the old ones. It is this menace not only to freedom of thought, but to beauty and pleasure and picturesque living that is forcing the intelligence and the aesthetic emotions of the South into revolt. And it is this revolution of ideas that must inevitably produce the Southern novelist of the future.

IV

And so it would seem that the qualities which will unite to make great Southern novels are the elemental properties which make great novels wherever they are written in any part of the world: power, passion, pity, ecstasy and anguish, hope and despair. For it is as true in literature as in war that with the imponderables lies the real force. The universal approach is not without but within; and the way to greatness leads beyond manner, beyond method, beyond movement, to some ultimate dominion of spirit. Even style, the essence of all great literature, is not a manufactured film but a vital fluid.

And what does this mean, after all, except that

148

the South must look more to inward inspiration than to outward example? It is well to have an American outlook; it may be better to have what is called an international attitude of mind; but the truth remains that great novels are not composed of either an outlook or an attitude. Even a return to aesthetic values in fiction will not help us unless we have values more genuine and profound than purely aesthetic ones. And what will it profit a writer to look within if he has not accumulated an abundance of vital resources? It has become a habit in both English and American criticism to remark that the South contains a wealth of unused material for prose fiction, which means only that a sense of tragedy and heartbreak still lingers beneath the vociferous modern "programme of progress." Wherever humanity has taken root there has been created, it is needless to point out, the stuff of great novels; and this is true of the South in the exact degree that it is true of every other buried past upon earth. But it is even truer that wherever the predestined artist is born his material is found awaiting his eye and his hand. All that is required, indeed, for the novel would appear to be a scene that is large enough to hold three characters, two passions, and one point of view.

In the Southern novelists of the past there has been an absence, not of characters, not of passions, but of a detached and steadfast point of view. What the novel lacked was, not only clearness of vision, but firmness of outline. For even the treasure of the inward approach may be wasted upon a writer who does not possess the practical advantage of the outward eye; and it is essential that the look within should be that of the artist, not of the lover. If the Southern novelist of the commemoration period was submerged in the stuff of life and incapable, therefore, of seeing his subject steadily and whole, the fault was not in the material, but in the novelist's inevitable loss of perspective. To be too near, it appears, is more fatal in literature than to be too far away; for it is better that the creative writer should resort to imagination than that he should be overwhelmed by emotion. And so it is only since the romantic charm and the lover's sentiment have both passed away from the South that the Southern novelist has been able to separate the subject from the object in the act of creation. It is only with the loss of this charm and the ebbing of this sentiment that he has been able to rest apart and brood over the fragmentary world he has called into being. For this is the only way, it would seem, in conclusion, that great novels, in the South or elsewhere, will ever be written. This was the way of Fielding with English life; it was the way of Hawthorne with the past of New England; it was the way of Proust with his world; it was the way of Tolstoy or Dostoevsky with his universe.

BARREN GROUND

B ARREN GROUND," which was published in
1925, may be regarded logically as one
of the scenes from country life in a social
history of Virginia since the Civil War. Or it may
be considered, with equal logic, to stand alone, as
it does in my estimation, secure in its own weight
and substance. It was outlined, indeed, as the first
of my novels of the country, after I had completed,
and dismissed from my thoughts, the final volume
of my history of manners. The germ of the book
had lain in my mind for many years; but when at
last it had developed too vigorously to be ignored,
I felt that I had broken away, even more sharply
than in my earlier work, from well-established
convention.

Twenty-five years before, thrilled by a new sense
of vocation, I had resolved to write of the South
not sentimentally, as a conquered province, but
truthfully, as part of a larger world. I had resolved
to portray not Southern "types" alone, but whole
human beings, and to touch, or at least feel for, the
universal chords beneath regional variations of

character. Because I distrusted, with reason, the entire Southern scene in fiction, and, especially, the prevailing nostalgic note in which it was commemorated, I had tried, in youth, the long distant view and the unknown approach to my subject. But my roots drew me home. My comprehension of Virginian life and manners was a knowledge of the blood, as well as the brain, and instinct warned me that here alone could I break through the surface of appearances and strike some vein of fundamental humanity. In the act of writing my youthful stories of strange places, I had known that I must return to the familiar earth in which I was rooted and to the earlier fibres of my identity, which reached far down into a past that was deeper and richer than conscious recollection. It was not that I wished to come back to the picturesque or the provincial. On the contrary, I had learned that there are many facets of human nature and that the aspect we call the regional is only the universal surveyed from a shifted angle of vision.

While I have faithfully painted the colours of the Southern landscape, I have always known that this external *vraisemblance* was not essential to my interpretation of life. The significance of this book, the quickening spirit, would not have varied, I believe, had I been born anywhere else. Nevertheless, I felt that the scene in *Barren Ground* possessed an added dimension, a universal rhythm more fluent than any material texture. Under the lights and shadows there is the brooding spirit of place, but, deeper still, under the spirit of place, there is the whole movement of life.

For the setting of this novel, I went far back into the past. The country is as familiar to me as if the landscape unrolled both without and within. I had known every feature for years, and the saturation of my subject with the mood of sustained melancholy was effortless and complete. The houses, the roads, the woods, the endless fields of broomsedge and scrub pine, the low, immeasurable horizon— all these images I had seen with the remembering eyes of a child. And time, like a mellow haze, had preserved the impressions unaltered. They are the lighter semblances folded over the heart of the book.

But Dorinda, though she had been close to me for ten years before I began her story, is universal. She exists wherever a human being has learned to live without joy, wherever the spirit of fortitude has triumphed over the sense of futility. The book is hers, and all minor themes, episodes, and impressions are blended with the one dominant meaning that character is fate. They are blended by life, not imposed by the novel. Though I wrote always toward an end that I saw (I can imagine no other

way of writing a book), Dorinda was free to grow,
to change, to work out her own destiny. At the end,
the implicit philosophy may be summed up in a
phrase: one may learn to live, one may even learn
to live gallantly, without delight.

In *Barren Ground,* as in *The Sheltered Life,*
I dealt with a community in which the vital stream
was running out into shallows. Though they belonged to different classes of society, the one rural
and the other urban, these two dissimilar social
groups were both remnants of an older civilization, of a dying culture. The declining aristocracy
was as passive nowadays as the thinning stock of
the pioneers. Like other social orders and individuals, both past and present, they had outlived their
usefulness, and time, the arch-antagonist, was dis-
carding them. In the higher class, to employ an
earlier label, the spirit of adventure had disin-
tegrated into an evasive idealism, a philosophy of
heroic defeat. Among the more backward rural
group, fortitude had degenerated into a condition
of moral inertia. Yet this culture as a whole had
sprung from the oldest roots in American soil, if
we except the native roots of the Indian. Here, if
anywhere in our Republic, a writer might unearth
the raw stuff of American civilization, the beginning and, one is tempted to add, the end of American democracy.

But was this culture actually dying? Was the wasting malady incurable? Immediately, this question would present itself to the psychological novelist. For these people springing up from an exhausted soil were the remote shadows of a stalwart breed; they were direct descendants of the Scotch-Irish and the English conquerors of the wilderness. Against the hostile elements of climate, drought, poverty, sterile soil, their only weapon had been some deep instinct for survival. This instinct, it is true, owed less to the attribute of courage than it owed to an innate capacity to exist without living, to endure without enjoying. For this also, I saw, was the Virginian strain, the American fibre.

And yet, so far as I was aware, this special rural class had never been treated in fiction. Several casual critics have referred to the characters in *Barren Ground* as "poor whites"; but the term is historically and socially inapplicable. The Abernethys, the Greylocks, the Pedlars, the Ellgoods had never slipped into the shiftless class of sharecropper or "poor white." As I explained in my first chapter, these farmers, though "land poor," as they say, owned, and had always owned, every foot of the impoverished soil which they tilled, or left untilled, on their farms. They belonged in a social unit which, though it has been consistently ignored alike by Southern literature and tradition, has borne a liberal part in the making of Southern history. In Virginia, this class was known, and is still known, as "good people," a label that distinguishes it from the aristocratic estate of "good families." Not a few of these "good people" were lineal descendants of English yeomen, mingled with a thin scattering of Germans who had arrived later on the flood-tide of immigration. But the ancestors of the Abernethys and the Pedlars had felled trees and built log cabins and withstood the red man on the Virginian frontier. Some of them had followed the westward trail of the Indian, and had won back, step by step, the vanishing border beyond the Shenandoah. They had fought in the French and Indian Wars and throughout the Revolution, and they had stacked their muskets for the last time at Appomattox. In pioneer days, they were the men in buckskin; they were the lone fighters; they were the sharp-shooters; they were the long hunters. And from the beginning to the end, they were inarticulate.

But their weakened progeny still held the freehold they had won from the wilderness or the savannahs. The grandchildren and great-grandchildren of the immigrants had established the order of small but independent farmers, which was presently to stand as a buffer class between the opulent gentry and the hired labourers. Because he was well-favoured, with a head that reminded one of an early apostle, Dorinda's father had taken a step above his humble station as a landless man, and had married the daughter of a Presbyterian missionary. Of this union of opposites, Dorinda was born, and the inherited conflict of types had kept her heart in arms against life. But she had inherited also a kinship with the solid earth under her feet, a long communion with the inanimate dust. Both the earth and the human breed were lean and depleted. Stubborn neglect, which followed the fury of war and the folly of Reconstruction, had wasted their energy, until animate and inanimate nature alike appeared resentful and sullen. Sterility, like an untamed evil, had sapped their power of renewal.

Many readers have remarked upon the time-sequence in *Barren Ground,* and upon the literal effect of the slowly changing years. What no one has perceived is that the elements of Time and Space are the dominant powers. From the beginning, I tried to evoke a background of unlimited space, "where the flatness created an illusion of immensity" and "over the immutable landscape human lives drifted and vanished like shadows." Behind the little destinies of men and women, I felt always that unconquerable vastness in which nothing is everything.

The sense of time is more difficult to achieve, and since it cannot be forced, it remains, I think, the most important problem that confronts the writer of fiction. In a long chronicle like *Barren Ground,* which records the significant events in a single drama of experience, success or failure will depend largely upon a natural impression of the passing days, weeks, months, years. This is made less easy when in so many of the years nothing has happened, when the drama is one of perpetual recurrence, of endless monotony. But, whatever the outcome, this movement of time cannot be arranged; it must flow inevitably from the theme of the story, which continues to obey the laws of an imaginary universe. Leaves budding, leaves falling, sun or snow, rain or dust, youth or age, life or death —this eternal sequence must place the tone of the narrative, and sustain the gradually lengthening effect of duration. Not the landscape alone, but the living human figures must reflect the slow rhythm and pause of the seasons, the beginning, the middle, and the end of man's warfare with nature.

In my earliest meeting with Dorinda, I saw her leaning against the whitewashed wall of the almshouse. I saw her vividly in the windless blue of an October day, and I felt that the place had a

meaning, or she would not have chosen it. Fate
had linked her with the almshouse, and that one
revealing incident was the origin of my novel.
Just as she brought with her, not only her own
name, but the inevitable title of the book, so she
gave me, in a single phrase, the vital clue to her
past. "Those summer evenings thirty years ago,
and this autumn day beside the wall of the poor-
house!" I grasped in that instant all that she was
trying to tell me. For the three years while she
lived actively in my mind, this sentence flickered
up again from my memory and ran, like a soundless murmur, under her story.

What I saw, as my novel unfolded, was a complete reversal of a classic situation. For once, in
Southern fiction, the betrayed woman would become the victor instead of the victim. In the end,
she would triumph through that deep instinct for
survival, which had ceased to be a negative quality
and had strengthened into a dynamic force. She
would be hardened by adversity, but hard things,
as she said, are the last to decay. And she would
never lose her inner fidelity, that vital affirmation
of life, "I think, I feel, I am." The only thing that
mattered was her triumph over circumstances.
Even the reclamation of the farm, which a few
critics have over-emphasized, was merely an episode. Systems of agriculture were unimportant be-

side this human drama of love and hatred, of passion and disillusionment.

As Dorinda conquered the land, which was, for her, the symbol of fate, so Jason surrendered through inherited weakness. The slow seasons, the blighted crops, the long droughts, the sudden frosts,—all this impotence of nature had afflicted his mind and body, as if it were the symptom of a mortal infirmity. His breed, unlike Dorinda's, held no immunity from the fatal germ of resignation.

A few of the minor characters were suggested, in part, by actual persons. Although I have not ever tried to draw a complete portrait from life, finding that exact copies of human beings invariably fade and die in one's hands, I have, now and then, filled in an outline by piecing fragments together. The nearest approach to full-length portraits in *Barren Ground* are the coloured matriarch, Aunt Mehitable Green, and Fluvanna, the servant and companion of Dorinda. There are living features, too, in Dorinda's father and mother, in old Doctor Greylock, in Geneva Ellgood, in Nathan Pedlar, in John Abner, in Mr. Kettledrum, the "mail rider," and in the horses, Dan and Beersheba. But it is worth noting, as we pass, that only a character we have treated objectively will submit to the firm handling of portraiture. External shapes, mannerisms, grotesqueries, all these may be touched off by a clever device or clean brushwork; but it is safe to assert that the genuinely created character must develop from its own embryo and pass through all the rudimentary stages of growth.

No sooner were the scenes and the figures assembled than they became more real to me, more moving and living, than persons and objects in the world I inhabited. It was ten years since I had first seen Dorinda in a fleeting glimpse, as a figure or a landscape is looked on, and then lost, from a train or a motor car. But, in all that time, she had continued to live on in some preserving atmosphere of the imagination. She had not only survived, she had lived some separate daily life of her own; she had become the centre of a universe that expanded. From a still figure beside a whitewashed wall, she had stepped out into the sunlight; she had put on identity. Every novelist is familiar with the potential energy that resides in imaginary persons, and with the way these persons rebel and follow their own courses when they are banished for long periods to the unlit places of memory. So I discovered, presently, that Dorinda was not the woman I had believed her to be when I first saw her. Though her name had not altered, she herself had grown more substantial and more human. In those ten years, which had washed over me as the tide washes over a beach, I found that we had changed and developed together. We were connected, or so it seemed, by a living nerve. I knew the look in her face, the tone of her voice, the high carriage of her head, the swift gestures that obeyed a thought or an impulse. I knew, also, the open country of her mind and the secret labyrinth of her unconscious motives. There was never the slightest hesitation in my handling of her speech or her behaviour. I was aware, through some sympathetic insight, of what she would say or do in any circumstances. From the beginning to the end, she breathed in my mind the air of probability.

And, in a lesser degree, because they are less prominent, this air of probability clings, in my vision, to the minor figures and even to the inanimate setting. The creative writer soon learns that when the central character has come to life, when the blood quickens in his veins, the pulses beat, and he breathes and moves, his immediate surroundings will awaken and respond to this sudden glow of animation. And of one fact I am assured, after a long and patient exercise of the craft of fiction:—the breath of life and the unerring sense of reality cannot be contrived or invented by any formula. They are beyond technique, for they must be distilled from some subtle essence of personality. The power to create life is the staple of fiction. When the novelist possesses this one thing needful, all else, or very nearly all else, may be acquired. But if he lacks this first principle, this primal element, he would be wiser to abandon literature and take up archaeology. For wherever there is life, there are infinite possibilities. But when either a book or a human being flattens out and turns to dust in our grasp, we have reached the dead end of both intuition and effort. The world of fantasy, like the world of matter, is for the living alone.

TUCKED away in some hidden recess of my memory, where it had lain unnoticed for many years, there was a novel with a setting in the Valley of Virginia. Thus far, I had written only of the Tidewater and Richmond. I was born in that section, and all my life had been spent there, except for the few years I had divided between New York and Europe. My mother's people had settled in the Tidewater in 1619 and 1634, and she was, also, one of a tribal multitude who looked back to that too virile progenitor, Colonel William Randolph, of Turkey Island.

But my father's forbears were among the stalwart pioneers in the upper valley of the James River and the fertile wilderness between the Blue Ridge and the Alleghenies. Glasgow, Graham, Anderson, they had first fled from Scotland to shelter in the north of Ireland, and then, when religious persecution still tracked them down, they had sailed from Ulster in search of a safer refuge among the savages of America. The original Glasgow homestead, built on a large tract of land, mostly wilderness, in Rockbridge County, is still standing, though it has been twice burned in part, and has suffered the even greater indignity of modern improvements. The place was named "Green Forest" because Glasgow means "greenwood" in Gaelic.

As a child and a young girl just growing up, I had spent many summers beyond the Blue Ridge; and it is probable that the seeds of this book were even then germinating in the soil of my mind. The Scottish ballads were as familiar to me as my alphabet, and far more beloved. My Aunt Rebecca, a wonderful old lady, and Scottish to the core, would sing these ballads, in her thin sweet voice, by the fireside of an evening, or, more thrilling to us, elders and youngsters alike, she would relate in serial form, since she was a born storyteller, all the adventurous plots of the Waverley novels, acting the separate part of each character and slipping, whenever the rôle required it, from her precise English into the exciting accent of Gaelic. Spurred on, at the age of seven, by an interrupted climax in "Old Mortality," I hunted for the worn volume inherited from my grandfather's library, and taught myself, with infinite patience, to spell out the words on the printed page. But I have never forgotten how the glorious adventures seemed to grow stale and flatten out when I read them in cold and faded print, deprived of the magical tones of my Aunt Rebecca's voice.

Years passed, and Aunt Rebecca, with her imposing generation, was almost forgotten. I had written both tragedies and comedies of the Tidewater and Richmond, when I apprehended, with the suddenness of all literary apprehensions, that a social history of the Commonwealth must, of necessity, include the descendants of those hardy Scotch-Irish settlers in the Appalachian highlands. The Great Valley of Virginia embraces the five smaller valleys of the Shenandoah River, the James River, the Roanoke River, the Kanawha, or New River, and the Holston, or Tennessee River. But the scene of *Vein of Iron* is restricted to the upper valley of the James, though I have been careful not to use the actual name of any place or person in that region. As I explain at length in my prefaces to *The Battle-Ground* and *The Voice of the People,* it was my original intention to depict such aspects of the Southern scene as I had actually known, and to avoid the romantic delusion, so prevalent in fiction at the turn of the century, that the South was inhabited exclusively by aristocrats and picturesque Negroes, who afforded what used to be called "comic relief" in the novel.

When, at last, I returned to this theme, I plunged

immediately into a state of total immersion. Few of my novels have interested or absorbed me so completely in the beginning, and I even enjoyed my researches, which fortunately left nothing more concrete than the essence of a moment in history. I read innumerable records of the frontier and frontier warfare. Sometimes I would search through several volumes in order to verify the state of the weather or the month of the year, and having verified it, I would dismiss it in a parenthetical clause. For the three full years while I was writing this book, I projected my consciousness, without effort, into that resolute breed from which my father had sprung. Having held fast through the generations, would this breed yield nowadays to the disintegrating forces in the modern world? Would that instinct for survival we used to call "the soul of man" be content to wear, for the future, the tarnished label of "psychology"? Would those intrepid Scottish metaphysicians, who had placed freedom to believe above freedom to doubt, and had valued immaterial safety more than material comfort, would they sink, in the end, under the dead weight of an age that believed only in the machine? Not in vain had my Aunt Rebecca instructed me, on the Sabbath, in the Shorter Catechism and the Westminster Confession of Faith. Not in vain, on the other days of

the week, had she sung the Border ballads and
related the Scottish legends. I had learned my
lesson well and long, though I thought I had forgotten it. Nothing remained for me to do but to
set the scene and attempt to analyze the primary
elements that composed the Presbyterian spirit
and the Presbyterian theology. And the chief of
these elements, or so it appeared in my examination, was the substance of fortitude.

In Ironside, I combined two mountain villages,
and so clearly was the setting visualized in my
mind that I was able to draw a map of imaginary
Shut-in Valley. I knew where every road climbed,
every house stood, every field spread, where every
hill swelled in the plain and every mountain peak
soared into the clouds. From the beginning, I had
known that I was engaged upon a family chronicle, that I was studying, not a single character or
group of characters alone, but the vital principle
of survival, which has enabled races and individuals
to withstand the destructive forces of nature and of
civilization. The ramifications of my subject would
lead me far back into the past, and, in order that I
might saturate my mind with the atmosphere of the
place and the time, I asked innumerable questions
of old and young, and I devoured every record I
could find of the earliest settlers in the Valley of
Virginia. When the book came to be written, I

found that these researches, which had occupied a year or more of my time, had contributed (if we except the general sense of security, the feeling that I could move about freely and safely in the scene and the atmosphere of the novel) exactly two pages of print. For, according to my dubious method of writing, it was as necessary to unlearn facts as it was to acquire them. What I needed, and what I had worked to attain, was a distillation of the past, not the dry bones and the decaying framework of history.

Not a few of these characters were suggested by an incident or an outline or even a gesture. In most of them a single living cell, or germ, was supplied by the anecdote or appearance of a "real" person. The merest fragment, it might be, was all I needed for my beginning; and in the case of Grandmother Fincastle, I pieced several of these separate fragments together, and so built up a figure of flesh and blood and spiritual fibre. I had known one or two Scotch-Irish grandmothers who might have sat for her portrait; and I am still receiving letters from her descendants who imagine they have recognized her features and have hastened, in one instance at least, to repudiate the likeness. The first John Fincastle may be traced back, in outline, to one of the earliest pioneers, a stout-hearted Presbyterian minister; and his picture also has been recognized, though not so far rejected. In Great-grandmother Tod, I have united two different persons, one a connection by marriage of my own great-grandfather. As a child of ten, she was carried off to captivity by the Shawnees; but it was another child who grew up in an Indian village to love and marry an Indian chief. The murder of the young chief by her two brothers, after the treaty that ended Pontiac's War, is one of the incidents recorded in the journals of the first settlers. In the later John Fincastle, I was trying to portray the fate of the philosopher in an era of science, of the scholar in a world of mechanical inventions. His return to an earlier spiritual age, and to the philosophy of Plotinus, is intellectually and historically accurate. Many of the pioneer ministers were men of intrepid spirit and intellectual vigour, and the transplanted Scottish mind was still nourished by metaphysics. In my childhood in Lexington, I had heard points of doctrine elucidated, though never argued, with all the subtlety of dialectic. Aunt Meggie, I had known intimately and remotely, in varied forms and fashions, from the Valley to the Tidewater; and I had known too, though only once, the imperfect original of Mary Evelyn.

So the family was grouped round a centre, and the chronicle was beginning, before I had put pen to paper. My characters, including the animals, even the pet ram, had gathered as obediently as the creatures in Noah's ark. I had steeped my mind in the setting of a mood, and divided my scene into foreground, middle distance, and historical perspective. All was waiting to begin, when I suddenly perceived that I had left my children out in the cold; I had provided everything but the right kind of roof. And, oddly enough, it was the roof alone that was making the trouble. I had seen the old manse in my imagination; I had seen the colour of the brick and the architectural design. I had seen every Fincastle, from Grandmother to little Ada and Horace, the hound, go up the rounded stone steps to the square porch, and pass through the front door into the hall, and then through the hall and the dining-room and the kitchen, out on the back porch and down into the yard. I had seen the pioneer oak and the rockery and the garden fence of white palings and the willow beside the little path that led down to the springhouse. But the house I saw so plainly was not the typical mountain house. It had its own peculiar plan, and its own sloping roof that drooped over the windows in the upper storey. Nevertheless, it was the old manse, and the Fincastles had built it. They had always lived under that roof, within those walls of weathered brick; and they refused obstinately to change their home, or even to go about their daily tasks, as long as they were threatened with eviction. Just as John Fincastle collapsed on my hands whenever I tried to change his name, so the whole family dropped dead at my feet as soon as I started to pull down the manse. So at last, in desperation, I told myself that an earlier grandfather, probably John Fincastle the third, had altered the original roof when he enlarged the house for his bride.

For the purposes of my theme, I should need, I knew, not only the force of tradition, as exemplified in Grandmother Fincastle and in Aunt Meggie, but the break with tradition which comes to Ada through Ralph and his frustrated ego. What I wished to do was to test the resistance of this vein of iron to outward pressure, and to measure the exact degree of its strength. Several readers have questioned the probability of Ralph's surrender to a moral code in which he no longer believed; but none of these readers, I am convinced, had ever lived in a strict Presbyterian community through the pre-war years, or felt the inexorable force of that Calvinist morality which Santayana has called "an expression of the agonized conscience." In his impressionable years, Ralph had been subjected to this agonized conscience (which at its best breeds inhibitions) in forms bordering closely on religious mania. Nor would this surrender of the broken will have been improbable in any long-established society, such as existed all over Virginia, and indeed over the entire South, where, until the post-war demoralization set in, religious precepts were still a formidable power for good or evil. In former years, I had witnessed one such instance in Richmond, and I had heard indirectly of several others. There may be a weakness at this point in my chronicle; but I think the flaw is owing less to the absence of probability than to insufficient analysis. Like other novelists, I suppose, I have my own favourite parts and passages, and those I felt, and still feel, most deeply in this book are the interlude on Thunder Mountain and John Fincastle's return to the manse at the end. Although Ada was nearest to me in many ways, I think the main strength of the book lies in the figures of the old Presbyterian grandmother and the old pagan philosopher. But all these people, including the Bergens and Mr. Midkiff, are so real to me that I can scarcely recall whether nature or I created them in the flesh. Otto Bergen, with his varied pets, was partly founded on a skilled cabinet-maker, who used to repair my furniture in Richmond; and he also had his sanguine smile and his dachshund, his canaries and his cages of white mice. Mulberry Street, with its good houses of

other days and its balconies of wrought-iron lace-
work, exists in fact, and so does the terraced hillside overlooking the canal and the river. Indeed,
I have taken few liberties with the actual plan of
the city I have called Queenborough. Here and
there, it is true, some architectural sacrifice to
progress or politics may have been restored; I
may have rebuilt a house or repaired a balcony or
replanted a tree; but, for the rest, I think my chief,
if not my only, offense has been in the renaming
of streets. One casual critic (the same critic, I suspect, who imagined that *Barren Ground* was about
the cultivation of land) has inaccurately described
Vein of Iron as "a novel of the depression." But
the truth is that the great depression, which occu-
pies only a few chapters, was, like the Great War,
an inevitable feature in any record of the time and
the place. Both the War and the depression were
there without my connivance; and it was impossible, in writing Ada's life, either to ignore them
or explain them away. But these things were
scarcely more than an incident in the larger drama
of mortal conflict with fate.

Technique has interested me since my early
years when, with only intuition and a natural ear
for words as a guide, I had groped my way toward a method. Consciously or unconsciously, I
was forming a style; but I felt that the style I

needed must have something more than mere facility. It must be alike elastic and adaptable and equal, on occasion, to the more or less serious emergencies of fiction. No good style can be uniform or expected to fit every subject, or indeed to fit every work by one author. I had seen too much excellent material spoiled either by a velvet style that would not give or by a fustian style that was fraying out. It is the fashion in criticism nowadays to praise the "invisible style." Yet this term is, I think, both far-fetched and indefinite. Style should be no more invisible than a transparent complexion which changes colour in response to the animation within. It should be recognized as a natural part of the organism, not as extraneous decoration which may be forcibly peeled off without impairing the whole structure. It was true, moreover, that, in the matter of style, as well as in the nature of substance, I was disposed by constitution to move always against the literary current. But if this knowledge ever entered my mind, I accepted it as unavoidably as one accepts sultry weather, and it failed to influence or even to retard the general tendencies of my work. If I was aware that I could never become one of the fashionable apocalyptic prophets of literature, I was aware also that I had little desire to be a prophet and still less to be apocalyptic. Even nowadays, when the kindly hearted are no longer unanimous in advising me to write in the manner of Thomas Nelson Page or James Lane Allen, and even my hopeful publisher has stopped urging me to "do an optimistic novel of the far West"—even nowadays, I am still obstinately facing the wrong way. For I have wished to do honest work, and I have found that to do honest work I must begin by not taking advice. "There were so many promising writers of your generation," a man of letters said to me recently in New York. "I wonder what has become of them." And I could only glance round at the altered scene and murmur, "I wonder."

Although I have had my loyal friends and critics, few persistent novelists, I suppose, have ever received in one lifetime so generous a measure of benevolent neglect. For all such double-edged blessings, I am able to say, since I have attained understanding, that I am not deficient in gratitude. To be choked with cream is, perhaps, the saddest fate that can overtake any promising writer. Not only was I spared this ultimate honour, but the lack of it has provided me with adequate space in which to take root and grow, without artificial grafting into a more popular stock. If I have missed many of the external rewards of success, I have never lost the outward peace and the inward compensation that come from doing the work one wishes to do in the solitary way in which one wishes to do it. It is true that I have seldom received prizes, but it is true also that I have seldom been obliged to return thanks. I wanted "a room of my own," and it was granted me. I wanted a pursuit that I might follow with interest between the cradle and the grave, and that, too, was allowed. As a beginning author, the odds may have been against me, but as an ending author, who has been saved from a sense of diminishing vitality, I think the odds are now even. For the old purpose, or illusion, is unimpaired. Still, I tell myself, after almost forty years of endeavour toward a single aim, that it is possible to reach below the semblance of fiction and grasp the verities of experience.

But to return to this novel. In handling an austere subject projected against a background of hills and sky, I felt that I required a closer adaptation of style. Sophisticated wit and sparkling irony must be drained away from this bare and steady chronicle of simple lives. And so the speech of the heart, not the language of the mind, must serve as the revealing medium for my narrative. After an excursion into civilized comedy, I was reviving the substance and the manner of *Barren Ground* and of those previous novels, which were written in ardent revolt from a literary convention that was formalized and inflexible. Years earlier, I had said that Southern literature needed blood and irony; and in writing of a social tradition that had become lifeless from immobility, I found that through an infusion of satire alone could the dry bones be made to appear animate. But these outworn husks of thought had never spread beyond the Blue Ridge into the Valley of Virginia. A living germ still survived in the long tradition of fortitude. Satire would have splintered back from the sober bulk of the Presbyterian mind and conscience. A natural vehicle, the grave speech of a spiritually proud and materially humble race, who disdained the artificial tongue of the sophisticated as heartily as they would have disliked the lusty tone so sedulously cultivated by Mr. Hemingway and his imitators,—this natural vehicle, perhaps the most difficult of all speech to translate into English prose, was, I soon discovered, the one inevitable expression for my novel.

For a generation style, as distinguished from manner, had been among my chief interests and my major preoccupations. I had worked toward a personal form which, however imperfect in the abstract, might become in time an appropriate instrument for my transcripts of life. An ear for cadences, as well as the history of criticism, had taught me that an unpruned style is a slovenly style.

But the search for the exact right word, it is needless to explain to any writer, is a perennial aspiration. I am, therefore, merely affirming a hope, not proclaiming an achievement. No one can comprehend more clearly than I do the stony road of failure that lies permanently between the dream and the actuality. Nevertheless, to the writer, the idea will remain always more real than the representation.

As long as a book has the life of reverie alone, it is possessed by the author; and through the stages of pre-natal development, it is attached by some vital cord to the writer's unconscious being. It is from this living matter that the structure, shape, nature, and external lineaments must be formed, either intuitively, as in my case, or by a deliberate act of the will. I knew, without knowing *how* I knew, not only the general construction but every small detail of my scene and my characters. I knew whence they had come and whither they were going, and that the imaginary world about them contained ample room in which they might move and turn and walk forward or backward. And I knew, also, what these people required of me if I expected them to stay alive in my hands. The point of view must be clear, straight, and restricted, as in so many of my novels, to two angles of vision. From the begin-

ning to the end, the events must be registered
either in the mind of Ada or in the mind of John
Fincastle. The eyes of youth must look on life
through the courage of emotion, while the eyes of
age regarded it through that fortitude which wisdom bestows. Only once do I depart from this
guiding principle, and this is when, in the early
chapters, I encounter a technical problem. In these
chapters, I treat subjectively five different points
of view in the family group gathered before the
fire in the manse on a December evening. As I
used it, this seemed to me to be an innovation, and
I employed the device not only because, in my
creation of the Fincastle family, I needed these
reflective views, but, in a measure at least, because the device was experimental and daring. It
is the kind of experiment, as a friendly novelist
said to me of my section "The Deep Past" in *The
Sheltered Life,* that is either a triumph or a defeat, because it cannot simply fall short of its end.

The truth is that it took me months to enter completely into the mental processes of these five different human beings, from the old grandmother
down to the child of ten, and to immerse myself
in their separate moods and visions. After I had
written these chapters, I felt that there was little
left for me to learn about the inner lives of my
characters. For each point of view, it was neces-

sary to discover or invent an appropriate rhythm. Grandmother's retrospect moves with a slow, rocking vibration, as when one is reluctantly falling asleep, and grows fainter and farther away as drowsiness conquers. "Suddenly, without warning, descended upon her a sleep that was not sleep as yet. Her eyes saw; her ears heard; and in her stiff fingers the needles did not slacken. But she was immersed in profound stillness; she rested upon an immovable rock." And in the concluding sentence the five almost wholly metrical lines are followed by the sudden break of the partial line at the end, which "drops off," just as does Grandmother Fincastle:

> "Wéaving ín and oút of her bódy and sóul, and knítting her ínto the pást as she knítted lífe íntŏ stóckings, móved the famíliar rhýthms and páuses— nów—of the hóuse; and móved as a cásual wáve, as bárely a mínute's ébbing and flów, in the tímeless súrge of predéstinátion. . . ."

And so the stream of reverie flows on and downward, through the metaphysical consciousness of John Fincastle, the practical mind of Aunt Meggie, and the flashes of insight that illumine Mary Evelyn's reflections, until it finally ripples out in the staccato cadences of little Ada's fanciful musings. In this day-dreaming, as throughout Gen-

eral Archbald's meditation in *The Sheltered Life,*
I have treated the past and the present as co-
existent in time, and time itself as a subjective
medium.

If these backward flights required density of
atmosphere, the whole theme demanded prose of
a transparent texture. And it was imperative, as I
have said elsewhere, that this style should spring
naturally from the characters and the situation,
and should be divorced, so far as this is possible
in any work of the imagination, from the personality of the author. The substance, as well as the
contour, must show clearly through an envelope
that is inconspicuous in itself, and yet able to
transmit equally light and darkness. I was striv-
ing in this book for a way of writing that was strong,
terse, without extraneous adornment, and impec-
cably true to reality. Only in the interlude on
Thunder Mountain and the last journey of John
Fincastle back to his old home, where burial was
cheaper, does beauty break through, not as an objective aim, but of its own inward movement, and
submerge the naked structure of life.

From the first paragraph, this theme had been
woven, for me, of sounds—of blended sounds, of
ringing, of murmuring, of harmonious and disso-
nant sounds. In the same way, but less emphati-
cally, I had felt that *The Sheltered Life* was shot

through with scents and colours, that *The Romantic Comedians* was composed of rippling lights, and *They Stooped to Folly* of laughing animation. In the very beginning of *Vein of Iron,* the rhythm tightens and moves swiftly, to the patter of running feet. Yet, so far as I am aware, Mr. Carl Van Vechten is the only reader who has observed the symbolic movement of my first paragraph, or observing it, has taken the trouble to record his observation in writing. Still, this is scarcely fair, since many readers and not a few professional critics have commented upon the variation of sound accompanying my chronicle.

All this, since it deals with the problems of writing and the architectonic design, does not begin until the substance in hand has assumed magnitude and proportion. With the origin of an idea, there is always the feeling that one is working in an imponderable medium, in some fourth or fifth dimension; but the minute we begin deliberately to break up, divide, and construct a pattern, we have dropped back among the physical unities. And though the physical unities may not lie at the heart of the matter, it is essential that a novelist should have command, not only of his material, but of its proper manipulation. Brushwork may not be the highest end of art, but it remains the solitary means by which an artist may arrive at the highest end. It is unfashionable nowadays, it is even considered a little absurd, to regard a work of fiction as a form of art. Nevertheless, the most favourable comment to be made upon any literary fashion is that it is only a fashion, which means that it will go out again as suddenly as it has come in. And from my unimportant point of view, only a form of art appears in a certain measure to be worthy of the dedicated service of forty years.

Novels of the City

What was time itself but the bloom, the sheath enfolding experience? Within time, and within time alone, there was life—the gleam, the quiver, the heartbeat, the immeasurable joy and anguish of being. . . .

NOTHING, except the weather report or a general maxim of conduct, is so unsafe to rely upon as a theory of fiction. Every great novel has broken many conventions. The greatest of all novels defies every formula; and only Mr. Percy Lubbock believed that *War and Peace* would be greater if it were another, and an entirely different, book. By this I do not mean to question Mr. Lubbock's critical insight. *The Craft of Fiction* is the best work in its limited field, and it may be studied to advantage by any novelist. In the first chapters there is a masterly analysis of *War and Peace*. Yet, after reading this with appreciation, I still think that Tolstoy was the best judge of what his book was about and how long it should be.

This brings us, in the beginning, to the most sensitive, and, therefore, the most controversial, point in the criticism of prose fiction. It is the habit of overworked or frugal critics to speak as if economy were a virtue, and not a necessity. Yet there are faithful readers who feel with me that a good novel cannot be too long or a bad novel too short. Our company is small but picked with care, and we would die upon the literary barricade defending the noble proportions of *War and Peace,* of *The Brothers Karamazov,* of *Clarissa Harlowe* in eight volumes, of *Tom Jones,* of *David Copperfield,* of *The Chronicles of Barsetshire,* of *A la Recherche du Temps Perdu,* of *Le Vicomte de Bragelonne.* Tennyson was with us when he said he had no criticism to make of *Clarissa,* except that it might have been longer.

The true novel (I am not concerned with the run-of-the-mill variety) is, like pure poetry, an act of birth, not a device or an invention. It awaits its own time and has its own way to be born, and it cannot, by scientific methods, be pushed into the world from behind. After it is born, a separate individual, an organic structure, it obeys its own vital impulses. The heart quickens; the blood circulates; the pulses beat; the whole body moves in response to some inward rhythm; and in time the expanding vitality attains its full stature. But until the breath of life enters a novel, it is as spiritless as inanimate matter.

Having said this much, I may confess that spinning theories of fiction is my favourite amusement. This is, I think, a good habit to cultivate. The exercise encourages readiness and agility while it keeps both head and hand in practice. Besides, if it did nothing else, it would still protect one from the radio and the moving picture and other sleepless, if less sinister, enemies to the lost mood of contemplation. This alone would justify every precept that was ever evolved. Although a work of fiction may be written without a formula or a method, I doubt if the true novel has ever been created without the long brooding season.

I have read, I believe, with as much interest as if it were a novel itself, every treatise on the art of fiction that appeared to me to be promising. That variable branch of letters shares with philosophy the favourite shelf in my library. I know all that such sources of learning as Sir Leslie Stephen, Sir Walter Raleigh, Mr. Percy Lubbock, Sir Arthur Quiller-Couch, Mr. E. M. Forster, and others less eminent, but often more earnest, were able to teach me, or I was able to acquire. Indeed, I know more than they could teach me, for I know also how very little their knowledge can help one in the actual writing of novels. If I were giving advice to a beginner (but there are no beginners nowadays, there is only the inspired amateur or the infant pathologist), I should say, probably, something like this: "Learn the technique of writing, and having learned it thoroughly, try to forget it. Study the principles of construction, the value of

continuity, the arrangement of masses, the consistent point of view, the revealing episode, the careful handling of detail, and the fatal pitfalls of dialogue. Then, having mastered, if possible, every
rule of thumb, dismiss it into the labyrinth of the
memory. Leave it there to make its own signals and
flash its own warnings. The sensitive feeling, "this
is not right" or "something ought to be different"
will prove that these signals are working. Or, perhaps, this inner voice may be only the sounder instinct of the born novelist.

The truth is that I began being a novelist, as
naturally as I began talking or walking, so early
that I cannot remember when the impulse first
seized me. Far back in my childhood, before I
had learned the letters of the alphabet, a character
named Little Willie wandered into the country of
my mind, just as every other major character in my
novels has strolled across my mental horizon when
I was not expecting him, when I was not even
thinking of the novel in which he would finally
take his place. From what or where he had sprung,
why he was named Little Willie, or why I should
have selected a hero instead of a heroine—all this
is still as much of a mystery to me as it was in my
childhood. But there he was, and there he remained, alive and active, threading his own adventures, from the time I was three until I was seven

or eight, and discovered Hans Andersen and *Grimms' Fairy Tales*. Every night, as I was undressed and put to bed by my coloured Mammy, the romance of Little Willie would begin again exactly where it had broken off the evening before. In winter, I was undressed in the firelight on the hearth-rug; but in summer, we moved over to an open window, which looked out on the sunset, and presently on the first stars in the long green twilight. For years Little Willie lasted, never growing older, always pursuing his own narrative and weaving his situations out of his own personality. I can still see him, small, wiry, with lank brown hair like a thatch, and eyes that seemed to say, "I know a secret! I know a secret!" Hans Andersen and the brothers Grimm were his familiar companions. He returned once, though somewhat sadly, after I had read all the Waverley Novels; but when I was twelve years old and entered the world of Dickens, he vanished forever.

In those earliest formative years Little Willie outlined, however vaguely, a general pattern of work. He showed me that a novelist must write, not by taking thought alone, but with every cell of his being, that nothing can occur to him that may not sooner or later find its way into his craft. Whatever happened to me or to Mammy Lizzie happened also, strangely transfigured, to Little

Willie. I learned, too, and never forgot, that ideas would not come to me if I went out to hunt for them. They would fly when I pursued; but if I stopped and sank down into a watchful reverie, they would flock back again like friendly pigeons. All I had to do before the novel had formed was to leave the creative faculty (or subconscious mind) free to work its own way without urging and without effort. After Dorinda in *Barren Ground* first appeared to me, I pushed her back into some glimmering obscurity, where she remained, buried but alive, for a decade, when she emerged from the yeasty medium with hard round limbs and the bloom of health in her cheeks. Thus I have never wanted for subjects; but on several occasions when, because of illness or from external compulsion, I have tried to invent, rather than subconsciously create, a theme or a character, invariably the effort has resulted in failure. These are the anaemic offspring of the brain, not children of my complete being; and a brood whom I would wish, were it possible, to disinherit.

It is not easy to tell how much of this dependence upon intuition may be attributed to the lack of harmony between my inner life and my early environment. A thoughtful and imaginative child, haunted by that strange sense of exile which visits the subjective mind when it is unhappily placed (and always, apparently, it is unhappily placed or it would not be subjective), I grew up in a charming society, where ideas were accepted as naturally as the universe or the weather, and cards for the old, dancing for the young, and conversation flavoured with personalities for the middle-aged, were the only arts practised. Several members of my family, it is true, possessed brilliant minds, and were widely and deeply read; but all despised what they called "local talent"; and my early work was written in secret to escape ridicule, alert, pointed, and not the less destructive because it was playful. There is more truth than wit in the gibe that every Southern novelist must first make his reputation in the North. Perhaps this is why so many Southern novelists write of the South as if it were a fabulous country. When a bound copy of my first book reached me, I hid it under my pillow while a cousin, who had run in for breakfast, prattled beside my bed of the young men who had quarrelled over the privilege of taking her to the Easter German, as the Cotillion was called. Had I entered the world by way of Oxford, or even by way of Bloomsbury, I might now be able to speak or write of my books without a feeling of outraged reserve. And yet, in the very act of writing these words, my literary conscience, a nuisance to any writer, inquires if ideas were really free at Oxford, or even in Bloomsbury, at the end of the century, and if all the enfranchised spirits who nowadays babble of prohibited subjects are either wiser or better than the happy hypocrites of the 'nineties.

From this dubious prelude it might be inferred that I consider the craft of fiction merely another form of mental inertia. On the contrary, I agree with those writers who have found actual writing to be the hardest work in the world. What I am concerned with at the moment, however, is the beginning of a novel alone, not the endless drudgery that wrung from Stevenson the complaint, "The practice of letters is miserably harassing to the mind; and after an hour or two's work, all the more human portion of an author is extinct; he will bully, backbite, and speak daggers." For being a true novelist, even if one's work is not worth the price of a cherry to public or publisher, takes all that one has to give and still something more. Yet the matter is not one of choice, but of fatality. As with the enjoyment of music, or a love for El Greco, or a pleasure in gardening, or the taste for pomegranates, or a liking for Santayana's prose, the bent of nature is either there or it is not there.

For my own part, the only method I have deliberately cultivated has been a system of constant renewal. If novels should be, as Sir Leslie Stephen has said, "transfigured experience," then I have endeavoured, whenever it was possible, to deepen experience and to heighten what I prefer to call illumination, to increase my understanding of that truth of life which has not ever become completely reconciled with the truth of fiction. I do not mean by this that life should necessarily be eventful or filled with variable activities. Profound emotion does not inevitably bear "the pageant of a bleeding heart." Several of the most thrilling lives in all literature were lived amid the unconquerable desolation of the Yorkshire moors. Yet it is doubtful if either the exposed heart of Byron or the brazen trumpet of D. H. Lawrence contained such burning realities as were hidden beneath the quiet fortitude of Emily Brontë.

Because of some natural inability to observe and record instead of create, I have never used an actual scene until the impression it left had sifted down into imagined surroundings. A theme becomes real to me only after it is clothed in living values; but these values must be drawn directly from the imagination and indirectly, if at all, from experience. Invariably the characters appear first, and slowly and gradually build up their own world, and spin the situation and atmosphere out of themselves. Strangely enough, the horizon of this real or visionary world is limited by the impressions or recollections of my early childhood. If I were to walk out into the country and pick a scene for a book, it would remain as flat and lifeless as cardboard; but the places I loved or hated between the ages of three and thirteen compose an inexhaustible landscape of memory. Occasionally, it is true, I have returned to a scene to verify details, though for freshness and force I have trusted implicitly to the vision within. And just as my scene is built up from fragments of the past, whether that past existed in fact or in a dream, so the human figures, though not one of them has been copied from my acquaintances, will startle me by displaying a familiar trait or gesture, and I will recognize with a shock some special blending of characteristics.

Frequently these impressions had been buried so long and so deep that I had entirely forgotten them until they floated upward to the surface of thought. Yet they were not dead but living, and recovered warmth and animation after the creative faculty had revived them. In the same way, halfobliterated images, events, or episodes, observed in moments of intense experience, will flash back into a scene or a figure; and this is equally true of the most trivial detail my memory has registered. For example, in one of the tragic hours of my youth, I looked out of a window and saw two sparrows quarrelling in the rain on a roof. Twenty years or more afterwards, a character in one of my novels looks out of a window, in a moment of heartbreak, and sees two sparrows quarrelling in the rain. And immediately, light streamed back, as if it were cast by the rays of a lantern, into the unlit recesses of memory, and I felt the old grief in my heart, and saw the rain fall on the roof and the two sparrows quarrelling there.

Because everything one has seen or heard or thought or felt leaves a deposit that never filters entirely through the essence of mind, I believe a novelist should be perpetually engaged in this effort to refresh and replenish his source. I am confident, moreover, that nothing I have learned either from life or from literature has been wasted. Whatever I have thought or felt deeply has stayed with me, if only in fragments or in a distillation of memory. But the untiring critic within has winnowed, reassorted, and disposed the material I needed.

Not until the unconscious worker has withdrawn from the task, or taken a brief holiday, and the characters have woven their own background and circumstances, does the actual drudgery of moulding the mass-substance begin. Even now, after the groundwork is completed and the subject assembled, I still give time and thought (brooding

is the more accurate term) to the construction. I
try to avoid hastening the process, and to leave the
invisible agent free to flash directions or warnings.
The book must have a form. This is essential. It
may be shaped like a mill-stone or an hour-glass
or an Indian tomahawk or a lace fan—but a shape
it must have. Usually a novel assumes its own figure when it enters the world, and the underlying
idea moulds the plastic material to its own structure. More deliberately, the point of view is considered and selected, though this may, and often
does, proceed naturally from the unities of time
and place, or from one completely dominant figure. In *Barren Ground,* a long novel, I felt from
the moment Dorinda entered the book that here
could be but one point of view. From the first page
to the last, no scene or episode or human figure appears outside her field of vision or imagination.

In *The Sheltered Life,* where I knew intuitively
that the angle of vision must create the form, I
employed two points of view alone, though they
were separated by the whole range of experience.
Age and youth look on the same scene, the same
persons, the same events and occasions, the same
tragedy in the end. Between these conflicting
points of view the story flows on, as a stream flows
in a narrow valley. Nothing happens that is not
seen, on one side, through the steady gaze of the

old man, seeing life as it is, and, on the other side, by the troubled eyes of the young girl, seeing life as she would wish it to be. Purposely, I have tried here to interpret reality through the dissimilar mediums of thought and emotion. I have been careful to allow no other aspects to impinge on the contrasting visions which create between them the organic whole of the book. This convention, which appears uncertain, when one thinks of it, becomes natural, and even involuntary, when the work grows, develops, pushes out with its own energy, and finds its own tempo.

Patiently, but without success, I have tried to trace the roots of *The Sheltered Life*. The background is that of my girlhood, and the rudiments of the theme must have lain buried somewhere in my consciousness. But I can recall no definite beginning or voluntary act of creation. One moment there was a mental landscape without figures; the next moment, as if they had been summoned by the stroke of a bell, all the characters trooped in together, with every contour, every feature, every attitude, every gesture and expression, complete. In their origin, I exerted no control over them. They were too real for dismemberment; but I could, and I did, select or eliminate whatever in their appearances or behavior seemed to conflict with the gen-

eral scheme of the book. It was my part to see that
the unities were recognized and obeyed.

It is only logical to infer that when a group of
imaginary beings assembles, there must be a motive, or at least an adequate reason, for the particular gathering. I knew, or thought I knew, that
no visitor had ever entered my mind without a
definite cause. These people were there, I felt,
according to a design, for a planned attack upon
life, and to push them out of the way would
spur them to more vehement activity. It was best
to ignore them, and this, as nearly as possible, was
the course I pursued. Sooner or later, they would
let me know why they had come, and what I was
expected to do. For me, they were already alive,
though I could not as yet distinguish the intricate
ties that bound this isolated group into a detached
segment of life. So this state of affairs continued
for several years. Another novel, *They Stooped to
Folly,* engaged my attention, while some distant
range of my imagination was still occupied by the
Birdsongs and the Archbalds.

Then, at last, *They Stooped to Folly* was finished, was over. Presently it was published; and
in company with all my other books that had gone
out into the world, it became a homeless wanderer
and a stranger. It had ceased to belong to me. I
might almost say that it had ceased even to interest

me. The place where it had been, the place it had
filled to overflowing for nearly three years, was
now empty. Were there no other inhabitants?
What had become of those troublesome intruders
I had once banished to some vague Siberia of the
mind?

It was at this crucial instant that the Birdsongs
and the Archbalds, under their own names, and
wearing their own outward semblances, escaped
from remote exile. While I waited, in that unhappy brooding season, which cannot be forced,
which cannot be hurried, the vacant scene was
flooded with light and animation, and the emerging figures began to breathe, move, speak, and
round out their own destinies. I knew instantly, as
soon as they returned, what the integral drama
would be and why it had occurred. The theme was
implicit in the inevitable title. Beyond this, I saw
a shallow and aimless society of happiness-hunters,
who lived in a perpetual flight from reality, and
grasped at any effort-saving illusion of passion or
pleasure. Against this background of futility was
projected the contrasting character of General
Archbald, a lover of wisdom, a humane and civilized soul, oppressed by the burden of tragic remembrance. The stream of events would pass before him, for he would remain permanently at the
centre of vision, while, opposing him on the farther

side, he would meet the wide, blank, unreflective gaze of inexperience.

In a sudden wholeness of perception, one of those complex apprehensions which come so seldom, yet possess a miraculous power of conviction, I saw the meaning, not only of these special figures, but of their essential place in this theme of age and youth, of the past and the present. They had been drawn together by some sympathetic attraction, or by some deeper sense of recognition in my own consciousness. My task was the simple one of extracting from the situation every thread of significance, every quiver of vitality, every glimmer of understanding. The contours were moulded. I could see the articulation of the parts, as well as the shape of the structure. I could see, too, the fragile surface of a style that I must strive, however unsuccessfully, to make delicate yet unbreakable. I could feel the peculiar density of light and shadow. I could breathe in that strange symbolic smell which was woven and interwoven through the gradually thickening atmosphere of the scene.

As at least one critic has recognized, the old man, left behind by the years, is the central character of the book; and into his lonely spirit I have put much of my ultimate feeling about life. He represents the tragedy, wherever it appears, of the civilized man in a world that is not civilized. And even the title, which I have called inevitable, implies no special age or place. What it implies, to me, is the effort of one human being to stand between another and life. In a larger sense, as this critic perceives, the same tragedy was being repeated in spheres far wider than Queenborough. The First World War was beginning and men were killing each other from the highest possible ideals. This is the final scope of the book's theme. The old man, his point of view, his thwarted strong body, saw the age pass by him. Not in the South especially; it was throughout the world that ideas, forms, were changing, the familiar order going, the beliefs and certainties. The shelter for men's lives, of religion, convention, social prejudice, was at the crumbling point, just as was the case with the little human figures in the story. . . .

While I am at work on a book I remain, or try to remain, in a state of immersion. The first draft of a novel, if it is long, will take two years, and still another year is required for the final writing. All this time the imaginary setting becomes the native country of my mind, and the characters are seldom out of my thoughts. I live with them day and night; they are more real to me than acquaintances in the flesh. In our nursery copy of *Gulliver's Travels* there was a picture which seems, when I recall it now, to illustrate my predicament in the final draft of a novel. Gulliver lies bound in threads, while the Lilliputians swarm over him and hamper his struggles. So words swarm over me and hamper my efforts to seize the right one among them, to find the right rhythm, the right tone, the right accent. But, here again, intuition, or perhaps only a flare of organized memory, will come to my aid. Often, when I have searched for hours for some special word or phrase, and given up in despair, I have awakened with a start in the night, because the hunted word or phrase had darted into my mind while I was asleep.

Nevertheless, it is the act of scrupulous revision (the endless pruning and trimming for the sake of a valid and flexible prose style) that provides the writer's best solace even while it makes drudgery. Every literary craftsman who respects his work has, I dare say, this same feeling, and remains restless and wandering in mind until, in the beginning, he has entered the right climate and, at the end, has tracked down the right word. Although my characters may develop traits or actions I had not anticipated, though scenes may shift and alter in perspective, and new episodes may spring out on the way, still the end shines always as the solitary fixed star above the flux of creation. I have never written the first word of the first sentence until I knew what the last word of the last sentence would be.

Sometimes I may rewrite the beginning many
times, as I did in *They Stooped to Folly,* and sometimes (though this has actually occurred but once)
a shorter book like *The Romantic Comedians,*
completely realized before pen was put to paper,
may ripple out, of itself, with its own energy.
Yet in the difficult first chapter of *They Stooped
to Folly,* I could still look ahead, over a procession of characters that had slipped from my control, to the subdued scene at the end, while the
concluding paragraph of *The Romantic Comedians* echoed the keynote of the book, and reflected
the ironic mood.

The final words to be said of any activity will
always be, I suppose, was it worth what it cost?
Well, the writing of fiction is worth, I imagine,
exactly what digging a ditch or charting the
heavens may be worth to the worker, which is
not a penny more or less than the release of mind
that it brings. Although I may not speak as an
authority, at least I can speak from long persever-
ance. I became a novelist before I was old enough
to resist, and I remained a novelist because no
other enterprise in life has afforded me the same
interest, or provided me with equal contentment.
It is true that I have written only for the biased
judgment within; but this inner critic has held up
an unattainable standard, and has infused a mod-

erate zest of adventure into what may appear, on the surface, to be merely another humdrum way of earning a livelihood. Still, to a beginner who is young and cherishes an ambition to be celebrated, I should recommend the short cut (or royal road) through the radio and Hollywood; and certainly more than one creative writer, in search of swift economic security, would do well to buy a new broom and to set out for the next crossing. But, incredible as it may appear in this practical decade, there are novelists so wanting in a sense of proper values that they place artistic integrity above the voice on the air, the flash on the screen, and the dividends in the bank. There are others who possess an unreasoning faith in their own work; and there are yet others endowed with a comic spirit so robust, or so lively, that it can find diversion anywhere, even in our national exaltation of the inferior. To this happy company of neglected novelists, the ironic art of fiction will reveal its own special delights, and may even, as the years pass, yield its own sufficient, if imponderable, rewards.

In looking back through a long vista, I can see that what I have called the method of constant renewal may be reduced to three ruling principles. Obedience to this self-imposed discipline has enabled me to write novels for nearly forty years, and yet to feel that the substance from which I draw material and energy is as fresh today as it was in my first youthful failure. As time moves on, I still see life in beginnings, moods in conflict, and change as the only permanent law. But the value of these qualities (which may be self-deluding, and are derived, in fact, more from temperament than from technique) has been mellowed by long saturation with experience—by that essence of reality which one distils from life only after it has been lived.

Among the many strange superstitions of the age of science revels the cheerful belief that immaturity alone is enough. Pompous illiteracy, escaped from some Freudian cage, is in the saddle, and the voice of the amateur is the voice of authority. When we turn to the field of prose fiction, we find that it is filled with literary sky-rockets sputtering out in the fog. But the trouble with sky-rockets has always been that they do not stay up in the air. One has only to glance back over the post-war years to discover that the roads of the jazz age are matted thick with fireworks which went off too soon. To the poet, it is true, especially if he can arrange with destiny to die young, the glow of adolescence may impart an unfading magic. But the novel (which must be conceived with a subdued rapture, or with none at all, or even with the unpoetic virtues of industry and patience) requires more substantial ingredients than a little ignorance of life and a great yearning to tell everything one has never known. When I remember Defoe, the father of us all, I am persuaded that the novelist who has harvested well the years, and laid by a rich store of experience, will find his latter period the ripening time of his career.

Transposed into an impersonal method, the three rules of which I have spoken may be so arranged:

1. Always wait between books for the springs to fill up and flow over.

2. Always preserve, within a wild sanctuary, an inaccessible valley of reveries.

3. Always, and as far as it is possible, endeavour to touch life on every side; but keep the central vision of the mind, the inmost light, untouched and untouchable.

In my modest way, these rules have helped me, not only to pursue the one calling for which I was designed alike by character and inclination, but even to enjoy the prolonged study of a world that, as the sardonic insight of Henry Adams perceived, no "sensitive and timid natures could regard without a shudder."

THE ROMANTIC COMEDIANS

THIS tragicomedy of a happiness-hunter was written, as an experiment, for my private diversion. Usually, my characters, even the least of them, are born of unrest; but life had no sooner pushed the figure of Judge Honeywell into my mind than his biography bubbled over with an effortless joy. Although the style is that of the vignette, and necessarily circumscribed, I feel that the technique I used was the only possible choice. Yet the word "choice" is not precise, since the act of selection or elimination was absent from the beginning. At the risk of appearing over-enthusiastic about my own, I may confess that, in my opinion, this novel is one of those happy marriages of form and idea which could not have been different.

In my work as a whole *The Romantic Comedians* has, and I think merits, a special, if narrow, niche of its own. It was the first of three comedies, or tragicomedies, that I had placed in my Queenborough in Virginia. For this trilogy, I felt that I required the distilled essence of all Virginia cities rather than the speaking likeness of one. The last thing I wished to do was to transfix the wings of my comic spirit and pin them down to an existence in fact. It is true that those of my fellow-citizens who have read my novels appear to recognize not only the place, but, with far less reason, or, indeed with no reason whatever, the people as well. They have, with a charitableness for which I am grateful, either ascribed the actuality to me or ascribed me to the actuality, whenever they have felt so disposed. Nevertheless, I hasten to explain that my new freedom includes neither moral nor literary licence. All I ask for my background is the saving grace of anonymity. All I ask for the author of this trilogy is that inalienable right of calling things by their wrong names which is common to all mankind, though it would appear to have reached its highest expression in the Southern breed.

For the rest, it is only fair that a writer who is not writing history should be permitted to furnish his own scene and arrange his own chiaroscuro, undeterred alike by nature and circumstance. If in my social history I had been careful to call every spade a spade and every molehill a molehill, in this comedy of manners, I have not hesitated to call a spade a silver spoon or a molehill a mountain. When I was writing *The*

Romance of a Plain Man, I verified, with exhausting, and I now think unnecessary, fidelity every detail of my setting; and my realistic conscience sternly forbade me to turn a maple into a mulberry tree. But in *The Romantic Comedians,* I have not failed, whenever I have needed shade, to make two trees grow in my Queenborough where only one was planted before me in Richmond.

For I had come at last to perceive, after my long apprenticeship to veracity, that the truth of art and the truth of life are two different truths. In any case, I had wearied of external verisimilitude when it conflicted with the more valid evidence of the imagination. Sound psychology, I found, was more important, and incidentally more interesting, than accurate geography. And more important to the novelist than any science, or all the sciences together, was the discredited art of the novel. Thus, when the final volume of my social chronicle had gone out into an indifferent world, I turned, with a fresh impulse and a heightened sense of conversion, to *Barren Ground* and to my new creed in fiction. . . .

After I had finished *Barren Ground,* which for three years had steeped my mind in the sense of tragic life, the comic spirit, always restless when it is confined, began struggling against the bars of its cage. It was thirsting, as I was, for laughter; but it craved delicate laughter with ironic echoes, and it moved always upon the lighter planes of reality. As far back as I could remember, there had seemed to be a dual nature in my image-making faculty. Tragedy and comedy were blood brothers, but they were at war with each other, and had steadily refused to be reconciled. My perverse imp of humour was not sufficiently robust to thrive either as parochial relief or as the boisterous offspring of realism. Its native element was the air, not the earth, and I had learned long ago that its flight could not be broken to the pace of pedestrian facts. Since it wore an aspect we have agreed to call civilized, it settled, finally, in that vague penumbra of consciousness which embraces two hemispheres—the world of fantasy and the world of matter. . . .

This trilogy was begun in the summer of 1926, and thus *The Romantic Comedians* is not yet old enough to rise as a ghost from the grave and reproach me whenever I turn and look backward. Even that younger writer who fraternized so cheerfully with the comic spirit, is not, nowadays, a dead person. I not only recognize this book as my own, but I still feel that, good or bad, it was the best I could do with the material at my command; and I should not wish to change it if I were permitted to take it apart and put it together again. A few sentences, not more than two or three, have been altered in the revised version.

Judge Honeywell is a collective portrait of several Virginians of an older school, who are still unafraid to call themselves gentlemen. Nothing was taken entirely from my acquaintances; it was a matter simply of contours blended and characteristics exchanged. Yet none of this, it is needless to say, was a voluntary process. The man himself was complete and alive in every part when he first entered my mind. Not until I had known him more intimately was I able to perceive a familiar outline or attribute. But I had wanted a subject for comedy, and now, in my need, one was proffered me directly from the background and atmosphere in which I had always belonged. Even the bare structure of events was one that I had often dissected and analyzed. Given such a man, freshly widowed and cherishing the memory of a frustrated passion, placed romantically between the old love, which was safe, and the new love, which was hazardous, with public opinion firmly pushing him toward the past, and awakened impulse violently thrusting him toward the future— given all these ingredients of drama, the situation would inevitably spin its own tragicomedy.

A few of the other characters, also, were partly

suggested by "real" persons. Mrs. Upchurch, the repository of common sense, I had known all my life in various fashions of dress and identity. Mrs. Bredalbane (Heaven be praised for her!) was a living pattern of the wayward Victorian crossed on the wayward Virginian. I was brought up to regard her less as a literary inspiration than as a warning example. In my early youth her defiance and her fateful doom (for she left more than her double in the actual Queenborough) were described, in the sepulchral whispers of legend, wherever groups of aging gossips were gathered. For my immediate generation, she, or her sisters in unrefined conduct, had cast the flush of romance over the exciting spectacle of sin. I was the witness, too, of her more or less victorious return to society, after the post-war psychology had worked as yeast in genteel convention; and I observed, not without satirical humour, that the youth of the period regarded her scarlet letter less as the badge of shame than as some foreign decoration for distinguished service. Why is it, I speculated, while I brooded over this drama, which I now recognized as a morality play, that happiness-hunters travel perpetually on roads that are circular and lead back again to the beginning? Mrs. Bredalbane alone seemed to prove that much can be done with the pleasures of living, if only one approaches them with a mind swept clean of prejudice and illusion. As a twin sister, she was, wilfully or providentially, the antithesis of all the virtues that Judge Honeywell cherished:—moderation, dignity, reserve, equanimity.

Among my acquaintances in Queenborough there appears to be a general impression that Amanda Lightfoot was snatched bodily, with every feature and contour and posture exact, from our own social circle. But I have not ever, I repeat, borrowed wholly from life. Every novelist, I suppose, except the happy romancer, is assailed with letters from persons he has never seen, many of them unknown to him even by name, who have recognized themselves or other members of their family, or their friends or even their enemies, in his narrative. Such wide response proves, no doubt, the substance and vitality of fiction; but all figures that are instinct with animation, that have solidity and roundness, have been touched and moulded, I am convinced, by the imagination. Just as Mrs. Bredalbane incarnated the rare Victorian revolt against duty, so Amanda embodied submission to the awful power which governed that interesting era. And since Amanda's personality was not bold and hearty, but flat and mild, she existed, in Queenborough and elsewhere, more as a pattern of pure womanhood than as a being invested with the tribulations of flesh. Because her attitude was general, as well as commendable, she will be easily recognized by all those women who have survived the severe discipline of the great tradition. But she is, as such women have always been, more active by nature than one would imagine from the unbreakable glaze of her femininity.

In Annabel, I was portraying youth in arms against life. This is the aspect of youth with which I have always felt a sympathetic alliance, not modern youth alone, but perpetual youth, in its spirited challenge to circumstances, and its light-hearted revolt against the conspiracy of the years. Not a few readers have condemned Annabel (assuming illogically, after the habit of readers, that only "sympathetic" characters are worth writing about) because they disapproved of her attitude toward that other happiness-hunter, Judge Honeywell. Yet this verdict, I think, is unjust. The truth is that, in this novel, reckless youth, like reckless age, was little more than the result of a single troubled epoch in history. The upheaval of the post-war decade had disturbed the steady stream of experience, and from the shaken depths embryonic fragments of impulse had floated to the surface of consciousness. Everything was becoming—or so it seemed at the moment— nothing was finished, except the Great War and the great tradition. There was no immunity from discontent. The invincible good sense of Mrs. Upchurch was stirred, if not shaken away from its anchor of pragmatic morality. Although she distrusted temperament, and was vaguely suspicious of any aspect of pleasure that was not profitable as well, she began, in spite of her disillusioned intelligence, to wonder about the past and to speculate, even more darkly, over the ways of the present. To Mrs. Bredalbane, a confirmed hedonist, who was regarded in her earlier years as an anachronism left over from the dissipated eighteenth century, the new freedom had promised all the comforts of faith without its irksome restraints. Even Altrusa, the coloured cook, who was predestinarian in religion, but had a firm hand with a crisis, was not insensible to the sudden swing from Negro spirituals into the syncopated riot of jazz.

All these people were drifting figures in a scene and a situation which were as fluent as time. Yet none of them moved in a vacuum; all were linked together, not only with one another, but with the dramatic unities which they observed and obeyed. Their origin is obscure to me, yet I cannot find among them a formalized or a flat character. When I first saw them, they were full, round, animate, and capable of extension. There is space between them and their background; my arm stretched easily about them and felt them to be solid. For me at least (and I am writing as an author), this whole group, from Judge Honeywell to Altrusa, seem to have created themselves out of chaos. Any novelist of experience knows the difference between the artfully invented puppet, which smells a little of clean sawdust, and the subconsciously created human being, who speaks and acts in response to the springs of character, and is controlled by some arbitrary power we call destiny. And all these imaginary persons contained, strangely enough, an almost equal endowment of reality. Judge Honeywell was scarcely more convincing to me than was Altrusa, who existed in only a few paragraphs of the story. Yet I do not mean to imply, in this candid confession, that only *The Romantic Comedians* among my novels has seemed to me to create a world of its own that expanded in time and space. This is equally true of *Barren Ground,* of *The Sheltered Life,* of *They Stooped to Folly,* of *Vein of Iron,* of *In This Our Life,* and of *Virginia.* But in most of my other books, I have felt that some few major characters were composed of a richer substance or were more self-contained than the rest.

This small social unit, which existed in its own special interdependence, was related also to the mood and the mental climate of the post-war decade. Everywhere in the world outside old cultures were breaking up, codes were loosening, morals were declining, and manners, another aspect of morality, were slipping away. A whole civilization was disintegrating, without and within, and violence alone was strong enough to satisfy a craving for the raw taste of life, for the sight and savour of blood, for the brutal ferocity of lust without love. In Queenborough, where lip-homage was still rendered to the code of beautiful behaviour, the long reverberations of violence were felt chiefly under the surface. An increased momentum, a shriller vehemence, a wilder restlessness— these were the visible manifestations of a decayed and dissolving social order. The comic spirit, an enemy to unreason in any form, was still urbane, though its irony was suddenly spiced with malice.

There is always the risk in analyzing one's own work that too much stress may be placed upon merely technical values. I doubt whether the natural novelist ever thinks, before a book is finished, in the terms of a formula. If theory enters the act of creation, it is wrapped up in some unconscious assimilation of knowledge. A novel designed according to the strictest laws of proportion and harmony would be as vacant as a temple the deities have rejected. A rich and vital work can spring only from a rich and vital consciousness of reality;

and so it would seem to follow that the pure novel is the result, less of logical means than of the process known to the Aristotelian philosopher as "fortuitous spontaneity." Nevertheless, it is still possible to examine the completed work and to ascertain the method, either deliberate or intuitive, by which it was fashioned. For more than thirty years, I have studied different methods of fiction and problems of technique, yet whenever I sit down at my desk and take up my pen, I detach my mind from the working of every literary formula. Life and life alone is the power that controls the slowly evolving situation. In the present work, I kept steadily in view one or two evident points. Since I had never written a comedy of manners, the trilogy I had undertaken would be more or less in the nature of an experiment; yet I felt instinctively, and my reason confirmed this, that the form demanded a brief time-sequence, a limited scope, and a touch that was light, penetrating, satirical. The comic spirit may be wistful, but it is never solemn; a heavy-footed comedy, or tragicomedy, is doomed to disaster. Although the theme accumulated its own dramatic values, I worked with infinite patience over pattern and texture, until at last the adapted style seemed to me to fit the subject as easily as the glove fits the hand. What I needed, I felt from the beginning, was a style that was neither soft and spongy nor so hard and brittle that it would flake off into epigrams.

My one regret, if it may be called a regret, is that, to the hasty reader, the ironic overtones may seem, occasionally, to deny the tragic mood of the book. For there is tragedy in the theme, though it is tragedy running, like the "divine things" of Nietzsche, "on light feet." When I have said that there was no selection of medium, I mean simply that my selection was not deliberate, but unconscious. I knew, of course, that the theme must move swiftly, with its own laughing cadences, toward an end of gay disenchantment, while "all the tender little leaves of April were whispering together." It was, indeed, this concluding paragraph that accented the rhythm and placed the final tone of the book.

Although the setting is Virginian, the characters belong to no particular age or place. In Judge Honeywell, I have tried to isolate and observe the pulse of life, not the pattern of declining gentility, but the universal hunger for a reality that is timeless. If his happiness contained, like love, the seeds of decay, it created, like love also, the illusion of its own immortality. For, as one critic has remarked, "the story is the illusion of perpetual youth, and Judge Honeywell is man eternal."

I T WAS because I had had enough of tragedy, and enough, too, of pity, that for the moment, if but for the moment alone, my mind needed to bite down on some hard substance, on some core of life that was impervious to sympathy. This need would pass; but as long as it remained, I wanted amusement tinctured with irony. I wanted a faintly sardonic laughter. The First World War, though actually I had been well out of it, had drained me of feeling. Until my inner springs filled again, I felt that I must turn to experiment and revolt.

Never before this book came to be written had a disembodied *motif* presented itself to me in place of a character. In every other instance, the central figure of my novel had first strolled across an imaginary horizon, or emerged suddenly from some remote point in the perspective. Recently, however, I had been reading of mythogenesis in the evolution of mankind; and it was while the comic muse played over this vast area that I was visited by the idea of embodying one of the immemorial woman myths in a modern comedy of manners. But what special myth, since it must, of necessity, be special, would lend itself to such treatment? And where, among quick or dead moralities, might I stumble upon that particular fable? For I had instinctively perceived that the moral myth alone might linger on in a mental climate which so strangely united the craving for romantic adventure with the satiety of emotional disillusionment. If my chosen myth must be ancient and honourable, it must be also still living and active. The sting of its irony, I saw, must lie in the point of its truth. What I wanted, in fact, was a myth that had survived as an integral part alike of pagan legend and of Christian tradition.

Now, it is the peculiar distinction of all woman myths that they were not only sanctioned but invented by man. Into their creation have entered many of the major prejudices and a few of the minor prerogatives of the male sex. Women have been too much occupied with the serious business of life, with planning, contriving, scheming to outwit an adverse fortune, and tilling the fertile soil of man's vanity, to bother about so primitive a science as mythology. But even among the distractions of an arboreal social order, man found an opportunity, between the seasons of hunting and mating, to evolve a cosmogony that flattered his self-esteem, and to moralize, with increasing fluency but diminished flattery, upon the enigma of woman. The results of man's cosmogony have been public property from the beginning. At an early date, they had secured permanent habitation in that sheltered area of the mind where superstitions reside; and they have been long embodied in innumerable rubrics and rituals. Although, under the proverbially celibate tooth of time, man's conclusions about women have become less renowned, they remain suitably commemorated in those fixed opinions which we persist in calling masculine ideals and feminine intuitions. These, also, though subject to decay from within, are equally invulnerable to the years and chance, to enlightenment and the Darwinian hypothesis.

In some green Neanderthal sunrise, soon after man had aspired to walk upright, no doubt he peered into a silver stream and decided that he had been created in the Divine image. On the same occasion, or within a reasonable space of time, he concluded, with even better authority, that, in constructing his companion, the pattern of his Maker had not been followed quite so closely. Since that memorable decision, among the vivid fluctuations of faith and fact, masculine reason has clung firmly to the primal commandment: "He for God only, she for God in him." Owing to the practical mind of woman, who is able to believe anything that is useful, and to find anything useful that she believes, an idea, however uncomplimentary, becomes sacred to her as soon as the tentacles of her faith have fastened upon it. Much practice, indeed, has perfected her in the fine art of dissembling.

For the *double entendre* is older than Mr. James Branch Cabell. It is older, indeed, than the famous conflict of the sexes which has yielded so profitable a victory to psychological novelists. And woman, informed by some secret wisdom that there are four dimensions to sex but only one to sex relations, has prudently condensed experience into a pragmatic philosophy. When she addressed man as "my author and disposer," it was with a vaguely sinister air of meaning far more than she said, which, by pricking curiosity, first established her as an influence, and later exalted her as a literary inspiration.

As this final achievement is the only one that concerns us, we shall leave the ancient legends asleep in their flowery grave, and hasten to approach the two preëminent woman myths which have exerted a benign or evil influence over the English novel. The myth of woman as an inspiration occupied an immovable pedestal from Richardson to Galsworthy. Not until it encountered all the brave young men and the Freudian perils of the post-war years was it overthrown by the bold modern myth of woman as an impediment. Between these two major fables, a whole flock of minor myths flitted, as airily as the doves of Venus, over the passive female principle in literature. From Richardson, who constructed a world of two solids and one ideal, to Mr. Cabell, who weaves a fabulous territory of two illusions and one impediment, masculine inclination has varied, according to the quality of mind or the habit of body, between these opposite fields of vision.

We need not examine deeply before we discover that the myth of woman as an inspiration has many advantages, especially for the myth-maker, over the contrasting myth of woman as an impediment. The cult of an inspiration has always been a remote worship. Even a feminine inspiration does not insist upon blocking the way of adventure, after the indecorous habit of a feminine impediment. For an inspiration is scarcely more solid than an ideal; and an ideal, conforming to the law of atmospheric refraction, appears not only higher than it is in reality, but looms still larger and brighter in situations of danger. This exclusive worship, therefore, has never lost its safe and honoured position in masculine enterprise, particularly when they have led into the Arctic Circle or among tropical jungles. Moreover, it has not ever

faiied to provide a respectable, and often chival-
rous, excuse for the most exciting and sanguinary
warfare. But an impediment, being on the spot,
demands immediate lip-homage; and it is in the
faculty of lip-homage that men so frequently
prove themselves to be inadequate as lovers. In
love, as in legend, they have, with the exception
of a few impotent poets, preferred deeds to words.
And even the poets, involved in the severe exigen-
cies of verse, have found that, while an inaccessible ideal quiets the mind and assists composition,
an accessible impediment is disposed to breed far
too many bitter realities.

The earliest, and still the longest, commemoration in English letters of man's ideal woman is the
immortal *Clarissa: or the History of a Young
Lady*. Many seasons have come and gone since I
read these eight fascinating volumes; and should
life be sufficiently prolonged, I hope, in some spa-
cious latter years, to repeat that thrilling adventure. No abridgement, I feel sure, can do justice
to this substantial, vivid, and now slightly ridiculous novel. Although Clarissa was not the first
completely living woman in English fiction, she
was the first completely incarnated feminine influence. Moll Flanders and Roxana are instinct
with vitality, but they can scarcely be called inspiring examples. They are far from genteel; they

are not even respectable. They belong, in fact, to that generous persuasion which men have created, with more courage than economy, in the lighter interludes of moral idealism. But the divine Clarissa, who clung as firmly to virtue as the modest Virginia clung to her clothes, remains, in spite of changing fashions, an extraordinary creation. Even if we admit the picture to be more remarkable as a reflection of man's sentimentality than as an analysis of woman's nature, this does not impair its value as the portrait of an ideal. Only the fecund imagination of man could have invented the moving scene in which Clarissa orders her coffin. After designing for the lid a broken lily just falling from the stalk, on a plate of white metal, she has her "palace," as she touchingly calls it, "placed near the window, like a harpsichord, and reads or writes upon it as others would upon a desk or table." This pathetic episode, which dissolved into tears the impressionable eighteenth century, is the crowning achievement of the most influential woman myth in the whole range of English prose fiction.

It is needless to pursue the romantic cult which, after so auspicious a beginning, dominated the English novel until Arnold Bennett and his contemporaries introduced the modern drab school. Fielding, the greatest of English novelists, was too

robust to amuse himself with the flimsy practice
of myth-making; but he was, also, of too warm a
nature, and too fond a husband, not to wish to pay
all possible honour to the wife of his youth. Although he still cherished the sentimental tradition,
fortunately he was as rich in humour as he was in
humanity. "No woman," remarks a character in
Amelia, "can be truly genteel who is not entirely
flat before." But Amelia herself is as round, as
ample, as smooth and glowing in texture, as the
Susanna of Tintoretto. She remains, notwithstand-
ing the web of sentimentality that enmeshes her,
one of the most living and lovable women in prose
fiction. Compared with her, the Amelia of Thackeray is as flat and scentless as a pressed flower. Indeed, the myth of woman as inspiration attains its
apotheosis in Thackeray and Dickens. Amelia
praying for George, "who was lying on his face,
dead, with a bullet through his heart," and Agnes
Wickfield with "her solemn hand raised toward
Heaven"—these are immortal symbols of the triumph of faith over fact. Fallen from its high
estate, damaged by time and chance, and debased
by ignoble adversity, this once supreme cult lingered on as a popular superstition until, at the end
of the First World War, the inferior myth of
woman as an impediment was born of an irregular
union between democracy and disenchantment.

Many masculine ideals have withered and died in the novel since Clarissa, hopeless of inspiring Lovelace to higher things, selected a broken lily as the emblem of her earthly career. Unhappily, the world is not what it once was; nor is the novel of manners; nor, for the matter of that, is an ennobling influence. If women are less tender than they used to be, they die less readily, even in fiction. Masculine adoration and feminine example have alike declined since the hero of *Children of the Abbey* exclaimed with rapture: "Estimable Amanda! I esteem, I venerate your virtue!" After Jane Austen, that delicate iconoclast, the romantic tradition was slowly blighted by frost and drought, and the literary portrayal of sex was no longer restricted to the classic postures.

More and more, the years since the First World War are becoming the dark of the moon for a number of exalted illusions. It is at least open to question whether women would ever have rebelled against their confining attitude had they not observed a diminishing humility in the novels written by men. At all events, after the War, male disillusionment with virtue, which had thickened like dust, invaded the whole flattened area of modern prose fiction. By some ironic reversal of the situation, woman, for so long the ideal of man, became, in a literary sense, the obstacle to all his higher activities. In a large majority of post-war novels, a woman or two women or even three women thrust themselves between almost every male character and some bright particular moon for which he is crying. And the credulous American public, fondly imagining that all the bold young men, especially if they have been to Paris and tasted absinthe, must know what they are talking about, has swallowed the latest Freudian complex as meekly as the serried rows of blameless ladies in women's clubs submit to the disrespectful berating of the newest British lecturer.

But to return to the most distinguished, if not the most youthful of our myth-makers, Mr. James Branch Cabell is fond of repeating, in his ingratiating way, that the desire for unattainable perfection is a masculine prerogative. When we read his books, especially the book that tells us something about Eve, but more about Adam, we are almost persuaded that to pursue the infinite and attain the finite has been the disillusioning experience of man alone. From Mr. Cabell's deceptive allegory (in which he proves with wit and learning that he has given over some thirty years to misinterpreting a special kind of woman) emerges man, the poet and the dreamer, in perpetual flight from woman, the devourer of dreams and poets. And it is not Mr. Cabell alone who resigns his heroes to this predicament. For these male authorities all converge upon the modest axiom that while man desires more than woman, woman desires only more of man. This is a theory so well established, and so firmly held in contemporary fiction, that, as far as I am aware, no man and few women have been rash enough to dispute it. Yet, like many securely fixed and well-thought-of opinions, it may be more vulnerable to attack than it appears. The capacity to pine for what is not is a privilege, or an infirmity, that is independent of sex. If man has dreamed of Helen and embraced Penelope, woman, condemned to a more prosaic lot, has sighed for fleet-footed Achilles while she was embraced by Odysseus. . . .

Thus I mused, in a whimsical reverie, until the ironic spirit at my elbow proffered me the almost forgotten myth of the "ruined" woman. Here, I perceived at a glance, was the subject I needed. Here was sentiment; here was chivalry; here was moral tradition; here was a well-honoured invention of man. Immediately, my perplexities vanished, and my inner obscurity was brightened by a flash of discernment. The rest, I surmised, would be effortless. I had only to sink my mind into the receptive mood, and the theme would unfold of its own dynamic volition. Already my characters were trooping into the light; and my comedy, as I saw it, would revolve about the ruined woman in three different periods of time and taste. Aunt Agatha, Mrs. Dalrymple, Milly Burden, they came in trippingly, each in her own age and fashion, bearing her own unalterable name. Even at that first meeting, I felt that Mrs. Dalrymple was the presiding genius among them. The light fell directly upon her; for she was the perfect bloom of that chivalry in which the Southern lady has so profusely flourished and fallen. The theme enchanted me from the beginning; and I soon found, after the background was furnished and the figures arranged, that the psychology of the ruined would provide its own comedy.

Nevertheless, there was work ahead for the critical faculty. As a matter of technique alone, my comedy must be confined, I perceived, within a curtly limited range. Both time and space must be circumscribed. A year, as in *The Romantic Comedians,* was the longest stretch of time that I could allow myself. Six months would be better; and this period I finally decided upon, after introducing the device of reflective interludes and soliloquies. Had it been possible, I should have preferred to reduce my time-sequence to the events of a single day. In this instance, however, the theme promised to develop too many variations. It would strike deeper and probe more acutely, I felt, than the

usual pure comedy. And all this striking and prob-
ing would supply, I hoped, constant animation and
movement. Moreover, the dramatic unities must
be sharply defined. While the characters must represent different ages of moral tradition, the scene
must be narrowed down to the immediate present,
and all extraneous details, by which I mean all details that did not touch, either explicitly or implicitly, upon the central idea, must be scrupulously pruned away. It was imperative, too, I understood, that sophisticated comedy should move
fluently against a background which was civilized.
Harmony was essential in the relation of the parts
to the whole. A single figure, a single object that
was out of value would destroy the tone and the
visible rhythm. I was living, day and night, with
these characters; I was carefully fitting them into
a general design. Every incident, every fragment
of dialogue, however spontaneous, must contribute
something, if merely an accent. It was true that
the overtones, if not the material, would be consistently light, and so much was pure comedy; but
the complete setting of the mood must be darker.

And then, as soon as the whole structure had
risen and the movement was well under way, I
discovered that the composition had developed beyond my original outline, and, of its own accord,
was assuming natural proportions. I began now to

envisage the story more broadly, as one of the novels of city life in my intended history of manners. Although the fable of the ruined woman would continue to provide the recurring *motif,* the scope of the narrative had widened to include other aspects of the time and the place. Obstinately, my subject refused to remain circumscribed by the limits imposed. Or it may be that my inner springs were filling afresh, and the increased source had extended my boundaries. Whatever the reason, the book before me, first conceived as a satire, was now unfolding as a serious study, with ironic overtones, it is true, of contemporary society. The reverberations of the War, and especially of post-war psychology, were audible even in remote Queenborough. So far as concerned that city (which I regard as the essence of all Virginia cities) the world victory had been won at the cost of a few lives and many illusions. The foundations of the old aristocratic order, overthrown two generations before by a nearer conquest, had never safely settled back on their corner-stone of tradition. The superstructure of faith was no longer invulnerable. To the dispassionate or cynical observer, it appeared doubtful whether the recently fallen standards, which had once so gallantly withstood material destruction, would ever rise again over the lost provinces of the spirit. In Queenborough, as elsewhere, the tone of manners rang hollow; there were many sounds but few human voices; men laughed more, but they smiled less, than they had done when codes were more strict and conduct simpler. Against this background of forsaken standards and distorted values, the amplifications of my theme must assume figures that were very nearly, though not entirely, symbolic of a world in confusion.

In Mr. Littlepage, as his character develops, we gradually approach the modern man who fears action, yet desires the things that only action can win. Confirmed in tradition, he moved uprightly in a vacuum of effortless motive. Externally, in a dwindling social order, he is defeated not by superior numbers alone, but even more by an infirmity of the will. Within, he hesitates and evades, but never completely loses his ground. And because he is inherently fair-minded, endowed with a sympathetic and generous nature, his impressions render the truest picture of an age in which he was fated to act the part of both victor and victim. His very inadequacy, which hinders him from taking either side as a participant in events, becomes an advantage when he is thrust into the place of a spectator. When his mind is held up to life, it mirrors the scene and the situation unclouded by vehemence. Even his urbane humanity, so unsuited to the period in which he has found himself, gives the identifying mark of validity to his reflections. Naturally, without my contrivance, he assumed the office of interpreter, in so far at least as it was possible to use the mind of a single actor as the stage for a drama so complicated. For it was essential that at every instant he should remain "in character," as one of the leading figures in the narrative. It was not sufficient that he should appear only as a medium reflecting the passage of time and the movement of circumstances. By being, if not by action, he must assert his identity; for the final ironic turn of the comedy hinges upon the secret confusion of his will with his emotions. It is necessary, therefore, that his interior world, with its surrounding anarchy, should share in the illumination his perceptions shed on external occurrences. His concluding episode with Mrs. Dalrymple reveals the individual human being as he has been moulded by inheritance, by tradition, by experience, and by the social forces through which his life is controlled.

In Marmaduke, on the contrary, we see the civilized man in despair of civilization, the artist in a society that classes art among the lesser utilities. Sensitive by nature, he wears, as a protective colouring, the buffoonery of truth. Though his point of view may throw an oblique light on the time, he does not, like Virginius, his brother, stand be-

tween the reader and the scene he observes. In the
two brothers, Virginius, the conformist, and Marmaduke, the rebel, are exemplified two opposite
views of the institution of chivalry. But Marmaduke's opinions, since he was handicapped by
veracity, as well as by the vagabond heart of the
artist, were inevitably tinged with the florid colours of his own personality. When the scene shifts
to his untidy studio in the ramshackle house overlooking the terraced hill and the canal, we perceive, as it were, the shabby side of tradition. The
convention of chivalry, like the ruined woman, depends largely upon its apparel. In better days, be-
decked with the trappings of war, its attitude was
spectacular. But after war, came the black crow of
post-war psychology; and the aristocratic tradition
lost the necessary support of moral idealism. Marmaduke, who had left one leg and the whole body
of his idealism in the war zone, had returned to
Queenborough chiefly because, as a cripple and an
indigent artist, there was nowhere else he could
go. After all, inherited ties were safer, when one
needed a life-line, than was the strained gratitude
of European democracies. One might despise one's
family as a unit, he had found, and yet respect the
members of it as persons. One might even despise
civilization, and yet seek its damaged shelter when
one needed a refuge. Embittered romantic as he

was, he had discovered that it was not only rational but logical to dislike human nature, and yet to like human beings. As a nice point in the quarrel over heredity and environment, one might contrast the conformity to type of Virginius with the eccentric variation of Marmaduke. To one side, sat enthroned the conservative forces of society and the moral order; on the other side were arrayed the international latitude and the unbridled temperament of an artist. Even so, we should be obliged to reckon with the influence of Victoria as a wife and of Louisa as an inaccessible virgin.

Martin Welding, the only other important male figure in the drama, was a member of that vocal generation which, if ever it were lost in fact, was in contemporary fiction but too easily regained. He suffered, not only from his share of post-war neuroses, which had intensified his fear of life and his innate lack of stability, but even more from a congenital weakness of fibre. Like many men of disordered sensibility and frail moral stamina, his very fear of the thing he desired, so often identified with his fear of women, exercised over his mind no less of fascination than of repulsion. He lived in a perpetual flight from love; and yet, owing to his physical attraction and his morbid susceptibility, he could not ever escape either from womankind or from his own vital hunger. In the end, we leave him still looking for a way out of reality, still building his dream hermitage in the cold and loneliness of the Himalayas. Although his symptoms are pathological, I found him both appealing and likable. I saw him as the victim, not of war alone, but, even more, of our successful mechanistic society. Had the war never been fought, he would have been in arms against life; he would have been defeated by the hostile forces of our civilized conformity. An inheritor of mental and emotional discrepancies, he was ready alike in mind and in body for that increasing modern epidemic which psychiatrists have dignified with the label "schizophrenia." In turning from Milly to Mary Victoria, his divided ego is instinctively seeking the mother in the lover and the earliest habit of protection in love. And in Mary Victoria, the incarnation of feminine self-righteousness, he finds both the protector and the devourer.

As for the three lost ladies of the comedy, each represents, in turn, a once popular style in American *mores*. I have, in my time, observed, with some interest, the different periods as they came and passed. During my early youth Aunt Agatha still lingered on as a surviving specimen of her variable, though permanent, species. Occasionally, as a child, I would pass the sombre house in which she lived immured; and though I had been warned

that it was improper to speculate upon the nature
of her affliction, I shared with my playmates the
vague impression that it was "something catch-
ing." A decade later, I had passionately admired
Mrs. Dalrymple as the reigning beauty of Queenborough; and I would sit for hours, on a cold
brownstone step, waiting to see her whirl by, at
first in a dog-cart with red wheels, and afterwards
in the very newest red motor car, with a white
chiffon veil streaming and spiralling over her
golden head. With Milly Burden, who had discovered that "being ruined is a state of mind," we
encounter immoderate youth in revolt, and the
latest, perhaps the final, version of the favourite
sport both of kings and of commoners. I have examined these varying stages so minutely in my
comedy that it seems superfluous to add anything
to this analysis. In passing, however, I may mention that Milly's mother, the desiccated Mrs. Burden, is the character whom I relished most heartily
—and, in particular, as she is presented, on a December evening, in a "flash-back" of consciousness.

Before I put pen to paper, the book was thus a
living organism in my imagination. For me at
least, it contained the principle of growth; it was
already endowed with vitality and movement. So
far as my command reached, I had control over

my figures, but my command did not reach far enough. By the time I was half through my comedy, one of the minor characters had resolutely advanced from obscurity. I had meant to keep Victoria in the background, to draw her, somewhat sketchily and flippantly, as a tiresome good woman; and I was even inclined to be a little annoyed when I found that she had, as actors say, "stolen" a chief rôle. It is true that I had wished her to go as far as simple goodness of heart, without any unusual beauty or charm or intelligence, can ever carry a woman; and my mistake seemed to be that I did not comprehend how great was the distance which simple goodness could cover. Two eminent critics, Mr. Stark Young and Mr. Carl Van Vechten, have been kind enough to include Victoria in the small group of difficult yet successful woman characters in fiction. By all the rules, they protest, she should have been tiresome, and yet she is never uninteresting. Gradually, as the book progressed, I found myself to be concentrating upon her, and to be trying, through her mind and heart, to explore the depths of the average woman of good will. The other women, old or young, were still as living, as wide awake, but their position and arrangement had altered. Instead of being the centre of the drama, they began to revolve about Victoria, and to move in her light. Especially is this the case with Louisa, the perfect club woman, whose friendship for Victoria rises, I think, to the highest point of my narrative. It is seldom in modern fiction that a friendship between two women, especially a pure and unselfish friendship, with both women loving the same man, has assumed a prominent place. Although such an association appears to be not uncommon in life, the novelist, since he is usually a man, has found the relationship to be deficient alike in the excitement of sex and the masculine drama of action. But more and more, in the modern world, women are coming to understand their interdependence as human beings; and without an example of this, a picture of our time that denied the place and the permanence of any such friendship would be wanting in complete veracity.

IN THIS OUR LIFE

WHEN I resolved, after finishing *Vein of Iron*, that I would not ever write another novel, I was reckoning without the unconscious will of the novelist. I might declare that the inner springs were drained, and had run dry. I might believe, or imagine I believed, that my long career as a novelist was now over. But I had forgotten that the severe discipline of logic rules in the actual world only less seldom than it rules in the lawless region of fantasy.

Vein of Iron was finished in April 1935. The book was published in August; and throughout the spring and summer my mind, or that branch of mind which is imagination, remained dark, and, to every appearance, empty. Then, suddenly, in autumn—always my fruitful season—vague, undeveloped shapes began to stir and move, and to thrust upward out of obscurity. Slowly, by their own instinct, against my expressed wish to write no more novels, these dim embryos assumed human form, and pushed on and outward, in obedience to some relentless blind motive. A new novel was forcing its way into the lighted spaces within. I might resent the intrusion; but I knew there would be no inward peace until I had ceased to resist, and allowed the unwelcome offspring to enter and take possession. For me, this would mean long endeavour, and perhaps failure. Nevertheless, I had learned from experience that rebellion would bring only inner disturbance. I was born a novelist, and I must die a novelist—or so it appeared. I had not ever known what it meant to be well. For many years, I had rarely known what it meant to be free from pain. The physical labour of writing would be irksome; the mental harassment might become a slow torture to oversensitive nerves. But I had found in the past that, though working could be anguish, not working might lead to a state I dreaded more than actual pain, and this was the lost restlessness of a thwarted mind. A book may not matter so much as the tiniest whirling grain of dust in the universe; but a thwarted impulse, working from within outward, may delude its helpless victim with an appearance of necessity.

Thus it was that I yielded. Reluctantly, I bought four dozen neatly sharpened new pencils. Reluctantly, I sat down, first at my desk, then at my typewriter. For me, by this time, my novel had become a reality, though it still remained, as Jung would say, "a reality *in potentia.*" I knew without knowing how I knew; I knew without knowing even *what* I knew. I heard the accent, the steady beat, of inevitability. Yet only in looking back have I been able to trace the pattern of the landscape or the winding turns of the road I travelled by intuition. . . .

In *Vein of Iron* I had tried to isolate and observe the living pulse of endurance, of that deep instinct for survival which has enabled man to outlast not only catastrophe, but even happiness, even hope. The external world had changed while I was writing, and the habits and the watchwords, if not the nature, of human beings were changing as rapidly. There was still more to be said in defense of fortitude, and there were other angles of vision. Although *In This Our Life* follows the general theme of *Vein of Iron,* the later book is in no sense a sequel. One of my generous critics has compared these novels to two movements of a symphony which might be entitled *Modern Times.* He continues, discerningly: "The line of inquiry is now apparent. It is to divest the human soul of its customary supports, to analyze it and refine it down to that indestructible core on which integrity rests. The Fincastles were undefeated; well, here is defeat, utter and constant. Pride is taken away. . . . Even courage is lacking, in its

ordinary sense, for Asa knows he is no hero.
. . . Yet he does not surrender. Why? What is the
essence, neither faith nor hope nor charity, that
can still hold a man together? . . ."

But the central figure in this novel is larger than
any individual character, for it embraces the interior life of a community. If I seem to labour
this point, it is because, to my astonishment, the
meaning has eluded a number of casual readers. I
had innocently imagined that the silhouette of
roofs and spires on the dust-jacket would convey
at least the bare idea that my outlook would be
more diffused than individual; and there is always
a shock in the discovery that, in print, one must
be brutally obvious if one wishes not to be mis-
construed.

The problem I had set myself was an analysis
in fiction of the modern temper; and the modern
temper, as it pressed round me, in a single community, appeared confused, vacillating, uncertain,
and distracted from permanent values. We are living in an age of disenchantment which, illogically,
resents disenchantment in literature. For I was
dealing less with a declining social order than with
a dissolving moment in time, with one of those
perpetually returning epochs, which fall between
an age that is slipping out and an age that is hastening in. Already, the potential tragedy of Eu-

rope could be felt by minds sensitive to vibrations. Yet on this isthmus of time, or narrow neck of eternity, while hostile forces thundered in the air, on the earth, or within our hearts, the few isolated free peoples, violent but unarmed, threatened with empty hands as they grasped frantically at the running shadow of happiness.

The scene, then, in this book is the intrinsic life of a community, as portrayed through the group consciousness. My major theme is the conflict of human beings with human nature, of civilization with biology. In this constant warfare tragedy lies, not in defeat, but in surrender. Time is presented always as flow, not as duration, and the stream of life should appear to move as the tide moves, ebbing and flowing, spreading out, or stealing in rivulets through separate minds, murmuring away and whispering back in subtle variations, like the sound of a recurring phrase in music, or the familiar repetition of winds and falling waves. For I was groping after that elusive significance of the profound within the simple. Thus I felt rather than thought that the fugitive illuminations must come through personalities long intimate with the scene and with the kind of life lived there in the past, as well as in the immediate present with which I was concerned. At least one well-intentioned friend has called *In This Our Life* "rambling," as if he were using the sharpened point of offense, when, by his criticism, he was, in reality, describing just that splintered light which I had attempted to shed on my narrative. In idea, if not in effect, I followed this wandering flow of thought and emotion, whether it was revealed on the surface, in conscious reflections and in eddying shallows and broken images, or whether, as impulse and sensation, a wave stirred and broke in the darkened reaches of the unconscious mind. Always the background and movement are those of the inner world. Though light and shadows fall directly, they fall inward, and external objects are perceived through that reflected light which is identity.

To condense this fluid state, and compress it into a solid substance, was beyond my power. To reduce these complex variations to a formula would be as difficult as confining the infinite ramifications of a social group within the compass of a microscope. My theme called for the thought processes of three different generations (any study of a family in any given society must do this), and it required, also, a careful and truthful treatment of two separate races, with their accompanying gradations of colour and of racial characteristics. Moreover, the light on the stream must sift, on one side, through minds that had been long a part of the place and the time, and, on the other side, through the fresh and vivid impressions of Roy, who is sharing the present while she is actively engaged in shaping the future. . . .

"Scientific civilization," admits Dr. Alexis Carrel, "has destroyed the life of the soul." And he adds: "For the first time in the history of humanity, a crumbling civilization is capable of discerning the causes of its decay." Although I should be among the last to deny that civilization, as Napoleon said of history, "is a fable agreed upon," I have learned, from both the past and the present, that nations decay from within more often than they surrender to outward assault. This is an admonitory truism; but it is a truism which we, in common with other races of mankind, have preferred to accept only on credit. We have refused to acknowledge that the disintegration of character is the beginning, not the end, of defeat, or that this weakening moral fibre is first revealed in the quick or slow decline of human relationships, and in the abrupt conversion to a triumphant materialism.

Always, as far back as I can remember, I have watched the play and interplay of attraction and repulsion in human ties. Entirely by accident, I happen to be the kind of person to whom other persons, sometimes total strangers, will confide life histories or secret dreams of the heart. This means simply that, like other novelists, I am willing to listen and to understand, whereas most human beings are absorbed in their own private activities. And in all these years of study, of observation, of reflection, of intense personal experience, I have found that too many otherwise normal persons are afraid of the word "happiness." I have seen, in my day, excitement, animation, wild happiness-hunting, and a too passive acceptance of things as they are. But I have not, anywhere, discovered a reason to deny Thoreau's profound saying: "The mass of men lead lives of quiet desperation." For this quiet desperation is the instinctive fortitude of the average man in his struggle with the forces of life, as well as with the brutal power of modern industrialism. In this book, I was depicting the lives of average human beings, not as they ought to be, but as they were, in the present moment of history.

Asa Timberlake mirrors the tragedy of a social system which lives, grows, and prospers by material standards alone. That Asa should be regarded as my idea of a failure by so many, if by no means the greater number, of readers proves the truth of Mr. Van Wyck Brooks's assertion that as a nation, or at least as a nation of writers, we are in danger of forgetting that character is an end in itself. Yet even that stalwart scientist, Dr.

Carrel, acknowledges: "Intelligence, will power, and morality are very closely related. But moral sense is more important than intelligence. When it disappears from a nation the whole social structure slowly commences to crumble away." One has only to read his book *Man the Unknown* to comprehend that, in the opinion of that foremost prophet, science alone cannot be trusted to save us. "Despite the marvels of scientific civilization, human personality tends to dissolve."

These utterances are both prophetic and apocalyptic; but I was concerned neither with preaching nor with prophecy in this version of reality. I was not trying to make men better or happier or more reasonable. I was merely rendering, as perfectly as I could, what I believed to be a partial truth of experience. It was not the whole truth or the only truth, but my special share of the whole truth and of the only truth.

As a child in Richmond, I was familiar with the work and the atmosphere, and, more especially, with the smells, of one of the privately owned tobacco factories. Of this place, I remember most distinctly the old men who sat on stools, writing in immense ledgers, or roamed stiffly about the stemming-room, with the authority of "floor managers." Although Asa Timberlake, too, was a child at this period, I have never failed to associate his future with these aging pathetic figures. In the end, after forty or fifty years of service, they were turned off, I heard, to beg or starve, when the factory changed ownership, with increasing profits, more than once, and was finally taken over by a brisk Northern trust. Such was the successful economic system which fostered our industries, and brought forth our vast American fortunes and a mushroom plutocracy. When I was so indiscreet as to inquire after the fate of one of these old men, I received the usual answer, "Oh, they were all superannuated. I never heard what became of them."

If Asa was the pivotal figure in this revolving group consciousness, Roy was the first character to push into my mind. As she appeared, she was saying over and over: "I want something to hold by. I want something good!" Hers is that special aspect of youth—yesterday, today, and tomorrow —with which I have always felt most sympathetic: that youth of the adventurous heart, of the everlasting search for perfection, of the brave impulse to hazard everything upon the first, or upon the last, chance of happiness. Roy was a part of life, with its softness and its hardness, with its strength and its weakness. She was not ever on the outside, waiting for something to happen. That final incident, with the stranger in the strange house, was actually the beginning of the book. As I went on, and as the pattern developed, I saw that this scene, important as it was to my meaning, might seem to have in the book's organic structure no part. I knew that more than one reader would find that meeting but casual. Yet in the end, I retained the complete episode, because of the illumination it shed on the major theme. I needed it for certain symbolic implications which could not, otherwise, be brought out in the narrative. In a narrow field, and in a small society, I was trying to reflect the disorders of a world without moorings, and driven by unconscious fears toward the verge of catastrophe. The significance of the lost Englishman, in part, was that he embodied a modern malady, an individual fear of life which was seeking to lose itself in a collective fear of death. "It is a psychological truth about war," observes a critic, who appeared to perceive my intention, "that is not to be confused with political or military truth."

For Roy, the meeting with this stranger who needed love more than she needed it, and was less likely to find it, served as a flare of light in the darkness of her own mind. When she went out into the windless dawn, after the storm was over, "She felt a sudden surprise, as if she had overtaken time, and were walking into a new age and a new

world." In the last scene, when she cries, "I want
something to hold by! I want something good!"
Asa answers: "You will find it, my child. You will
find what you are looking for. It is there, and you
—if not I—will find it." That this was a hopeless
ending had not occurred to me until Mr. Lewis
Gannett gently remarked on it. Ironically, I had
imagined that the book closed in the stern accents
of our unconquerable hope. Was this because
Asa's refusal to surrender seemed to me to be one
of those rare defeats that are victories, and to restore, paradoxically, the demolished convention of
the happy end?

Around Asa and Roy, standing together, the
other figures assembled by their own act and volition. Here, dying of cancer in his plethoric
eighties, is old William Fitzroy, the last great
Southern captain of industry. I have known him,
or his like, and I have known intimately Charlotte,
his wife, as well as Asa's wife, the more formidable
Lavinia. In my Negroes, I have come very near
to actual portraits. I have walked with Abel Clay
in his back yard, which he had transformed by
diligence and devotion into a flower garden. Minerva's people had belonged for a hundred and
fifty years to my mother's family. Minerva herself
is a blended portrait of two sisters, one dead, and
one still living in Richmond. With Parry, I have

trusted more to imagination; but I have known at least one of his sort, and he runs true to the individual variation from type. Since I cannot write naturally from observation alone, I had written the entire scene in the jail before I visited, and thus verified, that lugubrious satire upon Christian civilization.

For the rest, almost every town in the South has today, or has had yesterday, at least one completely selfish belle and beauty, who frequently bears, after a cherished Virginian custom, one, and sometimes two, proud ancestral names. I have been asked so often why I used the names Roy and Stanley for girls, instead of for boys, that I seize this opportunity to reply: The calling of girls by family names is a familiar practice in Virginia, especially when there are few boys to consider. Neither of these names strikes me as peculiarly masculine, because the only Roy and Stanley I have ever known were women. In this novel Roy was, of course, merely a convenient abbreviation of Fitzroy, and she had, it is safe to assume, been christened Lavinia Fitzroy in St. Luke's Episcopal Church. Oddly enough, I tried once to change her name to Rhoda, and she immediately went into a trance. One of the most curious facts in the making of fiction is the way characters select their own names, or are born

with them, and absolutely refuse to progress except on their own terms.

Because I was interested, above all, in the souls
of these people, I may confess to annoyance whenever the careless reader appears to regard the soul-
less little pleasure-seeker, Stanley, as the core of
this book. From the first page to the last, she is
treated objectively, and this may be the reason that,
to readers who do not look below the printed
page, she has seemed especially vivid. For me, she
remains always a part of the background, not
vital in herself, but with clinging tendrils which
reached out for support to the more real figures.
She is not evil; she is insufficient. She is not hard;
she is, on the contrary, so soft in fibre that she is
ruled or swayed by sensation. She embodies the
perverse life of unreason, the logical result of that
modern materialism which destroys its own happiness. It was her father who said of her: "I sometimes think she has no real existence apart from
her effect upon other people." That was the way
I meant to depict her.

In the preliminary sketch of *In This Our Life,*
as I wrote this outline in 1935, I had planned my
opening scene for the spring of that year. When
I came to my second draft, I found that the years
had moved on, with the quickened tempo of the
period, to April 1938. After this, my description

of the place, the time, and the weather became a contemporary record. It thus happened that I was not compelled to invent the long rains and the high winds at the end of that August, when Roy rushes out of the house in her final desperate break with tradition.

Although the style fell naturally into the more rapid prose of a transitional epoch, I wrote the first paragraph over for days, until it seemed to me that the movement of the entire book could be set to the beat and cadence of this opening rhythm. In a more impressionistic recurrence, I used the flight of pigeons, the flowing shadows on the pavement or on the grass, the different sounds of the rain or the wind in the leaves, the longings evoked by the scents of autumn or of twilight, and even Asa's half-forgotten recollections of the tobacco factory and the smells of the stemming-room.

These technical points can have interest, I am aware, only for other novelists. Bearing this firmly in mind, I was gratified when so many time-pressed reviewers, those theoretical economists of fiction, who contend that a book acquires merit by frugality alone, appear to have read *In This Our Life* with much leisure and care and understanding. All these, apparently, have agreed with me that the true and only purpose of fiction is the communication of ideas, of feeling, of vital experience.

Beyond this, a novel is entitled to be anything and everything, from a treatise on philosophy to an affair of the heart.

To be sure, among an inconsiderable minority of readers, I may still hear a faint continuing echo, which has lapsed over from the turn of the century. "If only you would write an optimistic novel of the Far West!"

"My dear publisher, if there is anything I know less about than the Far West, it is optimism."

"Why won't you try to write like Thomas Nelson Page, or even like James Lane Allen?"

"Why aren't you doing a Henry James novel?"

"Why do you not write rather more like Joyce?"

So runs my dream . . . But, after forty years of obstinate refusal to write "rather more like" Page or Allen or James or Joyce, yet, once again, I reply that never have I felt the necessity to imitate a book by somebody else, inasmuch as I have always before me the living model. And I may add: Surely, there can be no worse fashion in criticism than the practice of rebuking an author because he has not written another, and an entirely different, book, which he had no intention of writing, upon a subject of which he remains, whether happily or unhappily, ignorant. Just here, one cannot do better than answer in Virginia Woolf's pointed words: "Our gratitude largely takes the form of thanking them for having shown us what we certainly could not do, but as certainly, perhaps, do not wish to do." . . .

The first writing of *In This Our Life* was completed, and only five chapters of the second draft remained unfinished, when, in the spring of 1940, without warning, my heart failed me. With care, I was told, I might live for some years, or I might drop away, at any time, in a few weeks, or in a few months. If I hoped to finish my book, I must go very slowly, working from fifteen minutes a day to half an hour, and then an hour, but not longer. How I envied, then, those fortunate writers who had learned to dictate! But I had never been able to write except, behind a locked door, alone in a room.

Since *Barren Ground,* and even before, I had, invariably, made three separate drafts of a novel: the original sketch, very rapidly tossed together, for balance of structure, vitality of characterization, and in the effort to capture and hold a sustaining mood; the second draft for the sake of atmosphere and the arrangement of scene and detail; and, then, the final writing in a vain search for an austere perfection of style. This last novel would bring the long sequence of my history of manners from the period of 1850, when *The Battle-Ground* begins, to the autumn of 1939, when *In This Our*

Life ends. As I went on, I felt that I was assembling, in a single figurative pattern, all the varied yet closely related themes of my earlier and my later books. . . .

After spending a month in a hospital in New York, I went, in July, to a cottage I had taken at Castine, Maine, where I was able, by working not more than half an hour every morning, to finish my second draft. There remained, now, only the final, and to me important, task of smoothing and finishing. But, when I returned to Richmond in the autumn, after a second heart attack, I was not allowed to sit up at my desk or my typewriter. My problem had narrowed down to a single question: Should I ever be able, no matter how long I lived on, to write over again my whole novel? Five years of work had gone into this book, and the few persons who had seen the manuscript assured me that *In This Our Life* could stand as it was, without further revision. While I was very ill I tried to believe this; but, as I slowly regained strength, and after the entire book was in proof, and the galleys were sent to me, I braced myself to the effort of rewriting several chapters and a number of paragraphs. I shall always regret that I was not able to do my usual third draft, from the beginning. This story comes, I feel, to a pause, not to an end. My imagination still plays with these unfinished destinies; and I have promised myself that, if my strength ever returns, I shall write of Asa's hard-won freedom, and of its effect upon other lives, in a novel which I have already named, *Beyond Defeat.*

As with all my other work, readers have liked or disliked, very positively, *In This Our Life;* but few have remained merely untouched and indifferent. This is the case, I think, with all strongly individual personalities, whether in life or in letters. Temperament has more than reason to do with critical judgment. As Thoreau has said, in a phrase which Stevenson calls the noblest and most useful passage he remembers to have read in any modern author, "It takes two to speak truth—one to speak it and one to hear it." And, in another sense, is this not the way in which any living book must be read—any book, indeed, that contains the essence, or the extension, of a distinct identity? We find, in a certain measure, what we have to give, if not what we seek, both in the external world about us and in the more solitary life of the mind.

Bibliography

Bibliography

(*The Descendant*. New York, 1897.
Anon. The first printing has New York imprint only; later New York & London imprint. First binding does not have the author's name on the spine.)

(*Phases of an Inferior Planet*. New York, 1898.
Erratum slip at back regarding error at p. 194.)

The Voice of the People. New York, 1900.
First edition bound in tan buckram, with thin green pattern of oak-leaves and acorns. Copies in green cloth binding with Author's Edition stamped at the foot of the spine are a later binding. A reissue appears in a pictorial red cloth binding.

(*The Freeman and Other Poems*. New York, 1902. The DeVinne Press. Boards.)

The Battle-Ground. New York, 1902.
Published, March, 1902 on the copyright page. Frontispiece in color, from a miniature by W. J. Baer.

The Deliverance. New York, 1904.
Copies noted with either three or four illustrations. No known priority but copies in smooth red cloth are believed earlier than copies in rough red cloth.

(*The Wheel of Life*. New York, 1906.
Published, January, 1906 on the copyright page.)

(*The Ancient Law*. New York, 1908.
Published, January, 1908 on the copyright page.)

Bibliography

The Romance of a Plain Man. New York, 1909.

The Miller of Old Church. Garden City, 1911.

Virginia. Garden City, 1913.

Life and Gabriella. Garden City, 1916.

(*The Builders.* Garden City, 1919.)

(*One Man in His Time.* Garden City, 1922.
First edition so indicated on the copyright page.)

(*The Shadowy Third and Other Stories.* Garden City, 1923.
First edition so stated on copyright page.)

Barren Ground. Garden City, 1925.
First edition so stated on copyright page. Also advance edition of 500 copies in boards. Reissued by the Modern Library with a new introduction, New York, 1936.

The Romantic Comedians. Garden City, 1926.
First edition so stated on copyright page. Also 500 copies specially bound for presentation.

They Stooped to Folly. Garden City, 1929.
The first 3,000 copies were printed for "The Old Dominion Edition."

The Sheltered Life. Garden City, 1932.
Also 300 signed copies. First edition so stated on copyright page.

Vein of Iron. New York [1935].
First edition so stated on copyright page.

(*In This Our Life.* New York [1941].
First printing indicated on copyright page.)

Bibliography

COLLECTED EDITIONS

The Old Dominion Edition of the Works of Ellen Glasgow. Garden City, 1929-33, Doubleday, Doran and Company. Each volume revised and having a new preface.

The Virginia Edition of the Works of Ellen Glasgow. New York, 1938, Charles Scribner's Sons. With new prefaces by the author, 12 volumes (omitting the books hereinbefore printed in brackets), 810 sets only, signed.

CONTRIBUTIONS TO BOOKS

A Memorial Volume of Virginia Historical Portraiture, 1585-1830. Richmond, 1930. Alexander Wilbourne Weddell, editor. Introduction by Ellen Glasgow.

What Is a Book? Boston, 1935. Dale Warren, editor. Contains "Heroes and Monsters," by Ellen Glasgow.

Of Ellen Glasgow, An Inscribed Portrait, by Ellen Glasgow and Branch Cabell. New York, 1938, 109 copies only.

I Believe, edited by Clifton Fadiman. New York, 1938. Contains article by Ellen Glasgow.

CONTRIBUTIONS TO PERIODICALS

"The Dynamic Past," *The Reviewer,* March, 1921.

"The Novel in the South," *Harper's Magazine,* December, 1928.

"The Biography of Manuel," *The Saturday Review of Literature,* June 7, 1930.

"Flush: Portrait of a Famous and Much Loved Dog," *Books,* October 8, 1933.

Bibliography

"A Memorable Novel of the Old Deep South," *Books*, July 22, 1934.

"One Way to Write Novels," *The Saturday Review of Literature*, December 8, 1934.

"What I Believe," *The Nation*, April 12, 1935.

"Heroes and Monsters," *The Saturday Review of Literature*, May 4, 1935.

"Santayana Writes a Novel," *Books*, February 2, 1936.

"Elder and Younger Brother," *The Saturday Review of Literature*, January 23, 1937.

BIOGRAPHICAL AND CRITICAL MATERIAL

Ellen Glasgow: Novelist of the Old and the New South: An Appreciation, by Louise Maunsell Field. Garden City, 1923.

Ellen Glasgow, by Dorothea Lawrence Mann, Garden City, 1927. With Critical Essays by James Branch Cabell, Joseph Collins and Carl Van Vechten.

Ellen Glasgow: Critical Essays. Garden City, 1929. First printing indicated on copyright page. Essays by Stuart P. Sherman, Sara Haardt, Emily Clark.

BIOGRAPHICAL AND CRITICAL MATERIAL IN BOOKS

Page, Rosewell. "Ellen Anderson Gholson Glasgow," *Library of Southern Literature*. Atlanta: 1909.

Cooper, Frederick Tabor. *Some American Story-Tellers*. New York: Henry Holt and Company, 1911.

Kilmer, Joyce. "Evasive Idealism in Literature." *Literature in the Making*. New York: Harper and Brothers, 1917.

Bibliography

Overton Grant. *The Women Who Make Our Novels.* New York: Dodd, Mead and Company, 1918.

Sherman, Stuart P. *Critical Woodcuts,* New York: Charles Scribner's Sons, 1926.

Mims, Edwin. *The Advancing South.* New York: Doubleday, Page and Company, 1926.

Marble, Annie R. *A Study of the Modern Novel.* New York: D. Appleton and Company, 1928.

Cabell, James Branch. *Some of Us.* New York: Robert M. McBride and Company, 1930.

Cappon, Lester Jesse. *Bibliography of Virginia History Since 1865.* Charlottesville: The Institute for Research in the Social Sciences, University of Virginia, 1930.

Clark, Emily. *Innocence Abroad.* New York: Alfred A. Knopf, 1931.

Brie, Friedrich. *Ellen Glasgow.* Universität Freiburg, 1931.

Couch, W. T. *Culture in the South.* University of North Carolina Press, 1932.

Dabney, Virginius. *Liberalism in the South.* University of North Carolina Press, 1932.

Meade, Julian. "Ellen Glasgow," *I Live in Virginia.* New York, 1932.

Beard, Mary R. *America Through Women's Eyes.* New York: The Macmillan Company, 1933, pages 538-546.

Hatcher, Harlan. *Creating the American Novel.* New York: Farrar and Rinehart, 1935.

Hubbell, Jay B. *American Life in Literature.* New York: Harper and Brothers, 1936.

Bibliography

Johnson, Merle Devore. *American First Editions.* New York: R. R. Bowker Company, 1936.

Quinn, Arthur Hobson. *American Fiction: An Historical and Critical Survey.* New York: D. Appleton-Century Company, 1936.

Morrison and Commager. *The Growth of the American Republic* (Arts, Philosophy, and Letters), page 286. New York: Oxford University Press, 1937.

Van Doren, Carl. *The American Novel 1789-1939.* New York: The Macmillan Company, 1940.

Eggly, William H. "Bibliography of Ellen Anderson Gholson Glasgow," New York: *Bulletin of Bibliography,* 1940.

Millett, Fred B. *Contemporary American Authors.* New York: Harcourt, Brace and Company, 1940.

Monroe, N. Elizabeth. "Ellen Glasgow," *The Novel and Society.* Chapel Hill: The University of North Carolina Press, 1941.

Kazin, Alfred. *On Native Grounds: An Interpretation of Modern American Prose Literature.* New York: Reynal and Hitchcock, 1942.

BIOGRAPHICAL AND CRITICAL MATERIAL IN PERIODICALS

Marcosson, Isaac F. "The Personal Ellen Glasgow," *The Bookman,* August, 1909.

Overton, Grant. "Miss Glasgow's Arrow," *The Bookman,* May, 1925.

Rogers, Cameron. "Realism from the Romantic South," *The World's Work,* May, 1925.

Mims, Edwin. "The Social Philosophy of Ellen Glasgow," *Social Forces,* March, 1926.

Bibliography

Mann, Dorothea Lawrence. "Ellen Glasgow: Citizen of the World," *The Bookman,* November, 1926.

Richardson, Eudora Ramsey. "Richmond and Its Writers," *The Bookman,* December, 1928.

Rascoe, Burton. "Contemporary Reminiscences (Cabell, Ellen Glasgow)," *Arts and Decoration,* November, 1928.

Paterson, Isabel. "Rue with a Difference," *Books,* August 4th, 1929.

Haardt, Sara. "Ellen Glasgow and the South," *The Bookman,* April, 1929.

Dabney, Virginius. "A Prophet of the New South," *Herald Tribune Magazine,* August 25th, 1929.

Murdock, Kenneth. "Folly and the Ironist," *The Virginia Quarterly Review,* October, 1929.

Cabell, James Branch. "Two Sides of the Shielded," *Books,* April 20th, 1930.

Parker, William A. "Ellen Glasgow: A Gentle Rebel," *The English Journal,* March, 1931.

Young, Stark. "At Sheltered Valley," *The New Republic,* June 7th, 1932.

Young, Stark. "Prefaces to Distinction," *The New Republic,* June 7th, 1933.

Mencken, H. L. "A Southern Skeptic," *The American Mercury,* August, 1933.

Wilson, James Southall. "Ellen Glasgow's Novels," *The Virginia Quarterly Review,* October, 1933.

Villard, Leonie. "L'Œuvre d'Ellen Glasgow, romancière américaine." *Revue Anglo-Américaine,* December, 1933.

271

Bibliography

Delatte, F. "Le Sud des Etats-Unis," *Le Thyrse*, September, 1934.

Freeman, Douglas Southall. "Ellen Glasgow: Idealist," *The Saturday Review of Literature*, August 31st, 1935.

Delatte, F. "Ellen Glasgow," *Le Thyrse*, January, 1936.

Mims, Edwin. "Has American Literature had a Fair Deal in Great Britain?" *The Landmark*, May, 1936.

Jones, Howard Mumford. "The Virginia Edition of the Works of Ellen Glasgow," *Books*, July 24th, 1938.

Benét, Stephen Vincent and Rosemary. "Miss Ellen: A Rebel Against Regimentation," *Books*, July 24th, 1938.

Canby, Henry Seidel. "Ellen Glasgow: Ironic Tragedian," *The Saturday Review of Literature*, September 10th, 1938.

Adams, J. Donald. "The Virginia Edition of the Works of Ellen Glasgow," *The New York Times Book Review*, December 18th, 1938.

Wilson, James Southall. "Ellen Glasgow: Ironic Idealist," *The Virginia Quarterly Review*, 1939.

Cash, W. J. "Literature and the South," *The Saturday Review of Literature*, December 28th, 1940.

Jones, Howard Mumford. "Product of the Tragic Muse," *The Saturday Review of Literature*, March 29th, 1941.

Wilson, James Southall. "Ellen Glasgow: 1941," *The Virginia Quarterly Review*, Spring, 1941.

"Blood and Irony," *Time*, March 31st, 1941.

Brickell, Herschel. "Miss Glasgow and Mr. Marquand," *The Virginia Quarterly Review*, Summer, 1941.

Van Gelder, Robert. "An Interview with Ellen Glasgow," *The New York Times Book Review*, October 18th, 1942.